# Carolina Girl

# Carolina Girl

## A Writer's Beginning

by
Idella Bodie

**SANDLAPPER PUBLISHING CO., INC.**
ORANGEBURG, SOUTH CAROLINA

Published by Sandlapper Publishing Co., Inc.
    Orangeburg, South Carolina

Book Design by Barbara Stone

Manufactured in the United States of America



**Library of Congress Cataloging-in-Publication Data**

Bodie, Idella.
    Carolina girl / by Idella Bodie. — 1st ed.
       p.   cm.
    Summary: The author recounts her experiences growing
up in South Carolina during the Great Depression and World
War II.
    ISBN 0-87844-143-3
    ISBN 0-87844-140-9 (pbk.)
    1. Bodie, Idella—Childhood and youth—Juvenile
literature. 2. Authors, American—20th century—Biography—Juvenile literature. 3. South Carolina—Biography—
Juvenile literature.  [1. Bodie, Idella—Childhood and
youth.  2. Authors, American.  3. South Carolina—
Biography.]  I. Title.
CT275.B58227A3   1998
813' .54—dc21
[B]                                                  97-40937
                                                       CIP
                                                        AC

*For my granddaughter, Sarah,
who wants to be a teacher and writer*

~ ~

## ACKNOWLEDGEMENTS

I am indebted to my mother whose magical storytelling voice and loving nature kept my memories alive after all these years.

I would also like to express my gratitude to my editor, Barbara Stone, who was willing to get emotionally involved in this manuscript and to edit it with careful sensitivity.

Though the years many of you have asked the

My dear young reader,

Through the years many of you have asked me what my life was like growing up. Consequently, I have gathered memories, not just of my life but the lives of people in our small South Carolina town, to show you "the way things were" then.

I was born December 2, 1925, almost in the lap of the Great Depression. My hometown of Ridge Spring lies on what is called a "fall line." This geological line divides South Carolina's Up Country, rising to the Blue Ridge Mountains, and the Low Country, bordering on the Atlantic Ocean. When I left Ridge Spring at the age of sixteen to go to college, our country was fighting in World War II.

In writing about my childhood and growing up, I could hear voices from those years, especially my mother's. If memory failed to give me the words I needed, I worked at creating emotions remembered. All the people, places, and events are real.

Idella Fallaw Bodie

# Carolina Girl

# ~1~
# Pretend World

In our backyard, washerwoman Fanny plunged her arms into the sudsy water of a big tin washtub. Her body bent in rhythm—up and down, up and down—against the scrubboard. The soothing sloshing of the water blended with yard sounds: chickens *puck-pucking*, songbirds rustling oak leaves, the distant lowing of a cow. . . .

The year was 1930. I was five years old. In the *pretend* bedroom of my playhouse—the gnarled roots of a big oak—I leaned over a clothes basket, which cradled Fanny's "grand." Her eyes lay like black buttons in her velvet face. Suddenly her mouth primped.

"She's going to cry, Fanny!" I called out.

Fanny drew her arms from the washtub and wiped away frothy suds with her apron. From the rinse tub, at the other end of the wooden worktable, she pulled out a white scrap of cloth and wrung it out.

"Go in de kitchen," she said, handing me the cloth, "and get sugar out de bowl. Put it in de cloth and tie it up with your mamma sewing thread. De baby she like a sugar tit."

Careful not to stub my bare toes on a tree root as I left my playhouse, I dashed across the yard, past the four-o'clock bush to the back screened porch. The door banged behind me as I raced through the kitchen.

I could hear the clackety-clack of Mamma's treadle sewing machine. Any other day I would be with her. When she sewed, I made clothes for my doll. But today I had a real, live baby.

"Mamma—" I rushed up beside her and pulled open a narrow drawer. "I need a piece of thread."

Mamma stopped pedaling, picked up her scissors, and clipped the length I pulled from the big white spool. Then she gave the little black wheel on the arm of the machine a quick turn to start the pedal going. The clackety-clack picked up again.

In the kitchen I yanked a chair back from the table, climbed up, and reached across the flowered oilcloth to the sugar bowl. I spread out the scrap of cloth, dipped up sugar with my fingers, and put it in the center. Then I twisted the cloth tight, wrapped the thread around it, and tied a knot.

From the back door I could hear the baby crying. Little arms and legs flailed in the air. When I reached her, she was *all mouth*. I stuck in the sugar tit. She clamped her lips around it and sucked. I sat down beside her and put my finger in her hand. She clung to it with all her might. I began to sing to her the way I did to my doll.

*Hush, little baby, don't say a word*
*Mamma's gonna buy you a mockingbird.*

*And if that mockingbird don't sing,*
*She's gonna buy you a diamond ring.*

The sucking sound grew quieter and quieter until her face smoothed and her lips slackened around the sugar tit. I sang on.

*And if that diamond ring turns brass,*
*Mamma's gonna buy you a looking glass.*

*And if that looking glass gets broke,*
*She's gonna buy you a billy goat.*

*And if that billy goat runs away,*
*Mamma's gonna get you a one-horse shay.*

*Hush, little baby, don't you cry.*
*Daddy's gonna be back by and by.*

I eased my finger from her hand, now soft and loose. Through a root doorway I entered my playhouse kitchen. Oak leaf shadows danced in the sunshine across my table. Jar top plates and big spoons lay beside a dishpan filled with well water.

I was no longer five years old. I was the mamma. My baby slept in the bedroom of my house. Outside, my washerwoman stirred white clothes as they boiled in a big black pot. The smell of smoldering wood beneath the pot mixed with the odor of lye soap. Already scrubbed against a washboard, dark clothes waited in cold rinse water.

With a broom made of sedge from the fields, I swept my house while Fanny wrung out the dark clothes and carried them across her arm to the clothesline. She looped each piece over the wire. One at a time she flapped a shirt or pants out in the air like she was shooing chickens. Then she fastened it to the line with long clothespins.

I hummed to my sleeping baby and started cooking an acorn and leaf dinner for my husband who would be home soon.

## ~2~
# Family

I woke to the sound of angry voices coming from the kitchen. Mamma and Daddy were fussing again. Their voices grated against the soft morning light.

My sister, Louise—almost two years older—slept soundly beside me. Guy, who was nine, would be listening too. His room was closer to the kitchen. My stomach knotted.

The sound of dishes clattering against each other spread through the house with the smell of ham frying. In my mind I could see Mamma. She would be marching back and forth between the big black stove and the table.

Daddy let out a string of curse words. I covered my head with my pillow. I hated it when they fought. I loved them both. More than anything I wanted them to love each other.

Mamma had told us about eloping with Daddy when she was eighteen. "Maggie had my clothes ready to go to Greenville Woman's College," she said, "and I ran off and married your daddy." Always, she followed that up with "I wish Maggie had kicked me and made me go."

I knew Mamma wanted to be a school teacher like her older sisters, Lillie and Rosa. And Mamma had taught briefly. After she graduated from high school, she passed the required test to teach.

Mamma was born in the little town of Gaston, South Carolina, the thirteenth child in her family. Her mother died when she was nine, and she went to live with her older brother, Oscar, and his wife, Maggie, who didn't have children of their own.

Maggie and "Buddy," as Mamma called Uncle Oscar, owned a big two-story house in the Elmwood section of Columbia.

"They spoiled me," Mamma said. "Maggie never made me do a hand's turn. I had my own room upstairs. I read, took piano lessons, and played basketball."

I thought of Mamma's basketball picture in our photograph album. Three girls with their arms around each other wore blousy pants down to their ankles. The person who took the picture had cut off their heads with the camera. On the edge of the photograph someone had written "Feet and Bloomers."

Daddy was one of thirteen children too, but he was born somewhere in the middle. He grew up in Ridge Spring, where we lived. His parents, Grandma Ida and Granddaddy Rob still lived there. Everybody said I looked like Daddy's side of the family with my black hair and dark eyes. Once when I went with Daddy to get wheat ground into flour, the miller bent down to me. Even his eyelashes were white with flour.

"You're the spittin' image of your daddy," he said.

I liked to hear Daddy tell how his oldest sister, Aunt Tura, punished him when she was put in charge. She turned him upside down in the flour barrel.

"I'm sure you deserved it," Mamma would say and laugh. Her laughter rippled through the house when she was happy.

Daddy was eight years older than Mamma. They met when he came to see her sister, Aunt Frances, and Mamma had returned to Gaston for a visit. When Daddy was in a good mood, he still teased her about what a pest she was that day.

*BANG!* The slam of the back door pierced my pillow. It even made Louise jump. Soon I would hear our Model A Ford crank up and hightail it up the country road. Daddy left when he got mad, and he didn't tell anybody where he was going or when he would be back. Sometimes he was gone for days. I felt a sob building in my throat. I reached down by the side of the bed and lifted my doll from her cardboard cradle.

Cuddling her close, I whispered, "When I get married and have a family, I will never, ever have any fussing."

# ~3~
# Mamma's Girl

The familiar thick smell of Daddy's cigar lingered in the kitchen. It mixed with that of ham. Mamma's back was to me as I walked into the room. Her bobbed brown hair fell toward her face as she leaned to stoke the stove with wood. Sparks flickered, and she snapped the door shut with the curling wire handle.

I stood there watching her. I knew if I tried to speak, I would cry.

She turned toward me, her face softening. "Weezie still asleep?" she asked, using her pet name for Louise.

I nodded and pretended to rub the *sleepy dust* from my eyes.

"Cat got your tongue this morning?" Mamma pushed the skillet with the half-eaten flour hoecake onto the hot part of the stove to warm it up for me. "Hungry?"

I shook my head. Mamma read my mind. She reached out and hugged me to her soft body. "Shucks, don't worry about that daddy of yours. You know how he is. He'll be back before you can say 'Bobtail squirrel ginny.'" She smiled. "Besides, he's got to see about getting the cotton picked."

My throat grew tight, keeping my voice inside. Tears smarted my eyes.

"Here—" Mamma reached for the little cowhide chair hanging high on a nail behind the stove. "The oven's not hot. You can eat on the stove door."

I felt a bit better now that Mamma was taking down the chair for me. It had been her daddy's. He used it in his corncrib to shuck corn. He died when Mamma was sixteen and she treasured it.

Mamma held the chair out for me to see where the legs were worn off right down to the first rung. "All three of you learned to walk pushing this little chair around." Though I'd heard that many times, I looked before she set it down in front of the stove and opened the oven door.

Guy, Louise, and I all loved the little chair. When we fussed over it, Mamma grabbed it up in that fiery way she had of disciplining and hung it back on the nail. At nine, Guy was getting too big for the chair, but anything Louise wanted he wanted.

The stove door made a perfect table. I sat down and scooted my legs under. Mamma put my plate with the hoecake down in front of me. She had poured syrup over it and cut it up. Beside the hoecake lay a slice of cured ham from the smokehouse.

Suddenly I was "Little Two Eyes" in the story Mamma read us. I had two sisters. One had an eye in the middle of her forehead; the other had three eyes. Because I had two eyes like other people and was not different like my sisters, my family treated me mean. They even made me eat leftover scraps. One day when I was very sad, I went out on the edge of a field under a big tree and sat down to cry. To my surprise a fairy godmother appeared. She waved her wand and like magic a table of food was before me.

"Every day," the fairy godmother said, "you must come to this safe, warm spot, and I will have a meal for you."

I was feeling happy in my safe, warm spot when Mamma's voice broke into my daydream. "That brother of yours is already down at his peanut patch. Pete's helping him pull them up today."

I pictured Guy in the field working alongside our farmhand, Pete. Why did he have all the fun?

"Will you tell him to let me bag some peanuts?" I begged.

"Oh, it'll be a long time before he's ready to do that." She stooped and pulled the drip pan from beneath the ice box. Careful not to spill the water, she edged toward the back door and flung it outside.

"Then will you tell Louise to play with me?"

Louise appeared at the door and beat Mamma to an answer. "How many times do I have to tell you I'm not playing dolls?" She had already dressed in Guy's overalls. He didn't like her wearing his clothes, but she did anyway, unless of course she went to church or school. Everybody knew southern girls and women didn't wear pants in public.

"Dell"—giving a person a shortened kind of nickname seemed to be Mamma's way of showing she liked you—"if you're through, let Weezie sit there. You go get dressed. I want to put string up for my pole beans before the sun gets too hot."

"I don't have anybody to play with," I whined.

"Oh, run along." Mamma gave me a love pat on the seat of my nightgown. "You'll find something to do."

On the way to our bedroom I could hear Mamma trying to talk Louise into playing with me. I knew she wouldn't be able to.

# ~4~
# At Play

*Doodlebug, doodlebug,*
*Come out, come out.*
*Your house is on fire,*
*And your children will burn.*

I crouched under the front porch twirling a broomstraw in a hole and chanting the doodlebug song. Gently, I pulled up the straw. A plump hairy body clung to it. I held him over the tin can I collected them in and tapped the straw against the side of the can. He dropped off. I stuck the straw in another hole and sang the little rhyme. Soon the bottom of my can was covered with doodlebugs.

Our house sat on a hillside, the back side low against the ground and the front up high. It was cool under the house in summer. Sometimes I played "ice man" there with my cousin, Clyde, Jr., who was near my age. With a hammer and nail we picked out blocks of *dirt ice* and delivered them to imaginary families who lived along the edge of the porch.

A spider web brushed my neck. I pulled back and almost

touched a dirtdauber nest hugging a pillar.

Suddenly I'd had enough of coaxing doodlebugs out of their holes. I turned the can over and watched them scramble backwards. Some disappeared down old holes; others started new ones. I watched one use its tail as a shovel. As he shoveled, he walked backwards. Around and around he went until he was hidden beneath the dirt.

I crawled from under the house to yard sounds. Near the horse watering trough by the well a hen scratched and clucked to her biddies. They trotted after her in stiff little steps. I longed to hold one of them, but I dared not. If I tried, the mother hen would ruffle her feathers at me.

"Louise!" Mamma shouted from the garden. "You'd better stop that before you break your fool neck!"

Louise stood on the roof of a shed built against the side of the two-story asparagus packing house. She held our old black umbrella over her head. I watched her bend her knees and jump. Air fluttered the umbrella only slightly as she hit the ground with a thud.

She picked herself up and limped to the corner to climb back up. Seeing me, she called, "Okay. You wanted me to play with you. Come on up, and I will."

More than anything I wanted to be daring like Louise, but I was afraid.

"Come on," she urged, waving the umbrella above her head. "I know how to work it now. Next time I'm going to sail through the air."

I walked over to the corner where I saw her climb up. "I can't," I said, quietly rubbing my hands.

"Yes, you can." She put down the umbrella and stooped at the edge of the shed above my head. "Catch hold of that board sticking out."

I had on a dress, as usual, and though I was fearful of splinters, I did what she said.

"Now, pull up and put your foot in that crack."

She was leaning over, with her hand stretched down to me. I tried to work my foot into the crack she pointed out. The wood scratched my bare skin.

"Bring your other foot up to the next board sticking out, and I'll pull you on up."

"I told you, I can't," I complained.

"Just give me your hand." I could tell she was getting impatient with me.

I held onto the board with all my might with one hand and stuck the other up toward her. Before I knew what was happening, she had yanked me up. I lay sprawled on my side. I knew my panties were showing, but I was scared to move. I didn't want to roll off. Besides, my knee smarted from a scrape on the edge of the tin roof.

"For pity sakes," Louise said, taking hold of my arm, "sit up and scoot back."

I surprised myself at being able to follow her instructions even though my stomach did a flip. The roof had captured enough early-morning sun to be hot against my thin cotton dress.

"Now watch," Louise directed, "and I'll show you how to do it."

Like a trapeze artist in a circus, she poised on the edge, made a bow, whirled the collapsed umbrella over her head, and jumped.

Just before she hit the ground, air caught beneath the umbrella and fanned it open.

"Shoot fire!" she said, dusting off her overalls. "This shed's not tall enough." She tilted her head back and squinted up at the second-story of the packing shed.

"Mamma won't let you get up there," I warned. But then I remembered, Mamma hadn't stopped her from jumping off the shed.

Ignoring me, she threw down the umbrella and circled the asparagus house. The shed attached to the other side was used for the car, or the wagon if cotton needed to be kept out of the weather. It wouldn't be any taller than the one I was on.

Soon she was back. I heard her exclaim "Dog bite it!" before she called out to me, "Come on down. The game's over. There's no way I can get as high as I need to be. The ladder's not long enough." She turned to walk away.

"Wait!" I screamed. "I can't get down by myself."

"Oh, don't be such a baby. Go to the corner where you got up. Or jump down." She hurled the umbrella up onto the shed. It landed in a thump beside me.

I wouldn't be able to get down. I knew I wouldn't. I swallowed hard to get rid of the lump in my throat. I didn't want her to call me a cry baby. Then she would never play with me.

"Come help me," I called. I had turned around backwards and was trying to do what she said when I heard her laugh. Still giggling, she chanted, "I see China; I see France; I see Idella's underpants."

I jerked my foot back and yelled "MA–MA!"

Mamma came running from the garden, hoe in hand.

"She won't try to get down," Louise said.

"She's not as big as you," Mamma scolded. I knew she

meant as *old* because the three of us were near the same size. Malaria had made Guy small for his age.

Mamma tried to coax me down. Finally, she got the ladder from under the shed and leaned it against the roof.

When at last I was down, I got my doll and took her to our secret place in the privet hedge at the corner of the front yard. I told her stories and took her to visit my imaginary friends. We didn't stay long at Mrs. Jaques, who lived over by the spirea bush. She was so bossy—always telling me how to bring up my doll. I just stomped off.

That night, I woke to a thunderstorm. Rain thrummed on the roof. Lighting streaked across our windows.

I slipped from my bed and into Mamma and Daddy's room. Daddy had not come home. I climbed up by Mamma. She turned toward me and put her arm around me. Like two spoons in the silverware drawer we cuddled against the storm.

# ~5~
# Ranger

Guy washed his peanuts in a bucket by the well. Louise sat on a real horse saddle perched between the forked trunk of the big oak by the back door.

I was trying to sweep the yard with a dogwood broom. It always seemed so easy when I watched Mamma and Floride, the girl who worked for us. But my strokes looked like chicken scratches.

We all heard the car about the same time. It had to be

coming to our house; we lived at the end of the road. I threw down the broom and ran to the back of the house by the sunflowers for a better view.

It was Daddy. A rooster tail of dust trailed the Model A along the narrow road. The car whipped down the hill, circled the front of the house, and pulled up by the asparagus shed. I made a beeline toward it.

In moments Daddy stood holding the leash of the biggest dog I'd ever seen. He came almost up to Daddy's waist. The dog's thick brown fur had dark streaks tipped with silver. He looked like Rin Tin Tin, the dog in the picture shows.

I didn't realize Mamma had gone back inside until I heard her call out from the back door. "You can take that dog right back where you got him from. I'm not having him around the children."

Working his cigar from one side of his mouth to the other, Daddy stood, not saying a word. He lifted his hat and smoothed his black hair. Then he walked the dog over to the horse trough to let him drink.

I was glad Daddy was home, and I knew Guy and Louise were too. We weren't affectionate with him the way we were with Mamma, but I knew he loved us.

"Pete help you get the peanuts off the vines?" he asked Guy.

"Yes, sir." Guy looked up at him, squinting against the sunlight. "But he's pulling corn now."

"Let me check on him," Daddy said, "and I'll help you boil 'em." He stooped down to look in Guy's bucket. "Be sure to get all the dirt off."

He hooked the dog's leash on a chain hanging from an oak limb where he weighed cotton and headed toward the upper cornfield.

Mamma called out again. "Ya'll stay back from that dog. You hear?"

The second the screened door slammed, Louise took a step closer.

The well pully creaked as Guy drew up another bucket of water. "You heard what Mamma said," he told her.

"Well, he's wagging his tail," Louise quipped.

Even if I hadn't been taught not to pet strange dogs, I wouldn't go near this one. He had a fierce look about him. Anyway, we pretty well kept our distance until Mamma brought out a pan of cooked grits with grease drippings from the stove's warming closet.

"No telling when he's had anything to eat," she said as she plopped the food down in front of him. She didn't seem very happy as she headed back to the house.

We watched the dog gobble up the food—his wide feet planted firmly and his big jaws slapping with each mouthful. When he finished, Louise eased up to him and put out her hand. He licked it and wagged his tail.

"His name's going to be Ranger." Guy's announcement sounded like he thought the dog would stay.

The peanuts boiled in the big pot on the stove most of the afternoon. Finally, Mamma dipped a spoonful to cool. We each tasted one. As usual, they needed more salt.

After supper, when the peanuts had soaked long enough in the briny liquid and cooled, Daddy helped Guy drain off the water and bag them to sell. The two of them had a special way they held the filled bags by the corners and flipped them over and over, forming little twists on the outside corners. This kept the bags nice and tight.

Louise and I wanted to flip the bags, but Guy wouldn't let us. "Nope," he said. "You don't know how, and I'm not having you practice on my bags. I had to pay for them."

To keep us occupied, Mamma drew Louise and me out on the porch with a book. It was a good place to read . . . but I think she was also doing it to get away from Daddy. They weren't talking to each other yet.

With one of us on either side of her in the porch swing, Mamma cast her magic spell with her voice. Louise and I knew all the stories by heart, of course, but each time we listened as if we were hearing them for the first time.

The one Mamma read this time was "The Star Dipper." It was about a little girl who lived with her mother in a house in the woods. When her mother became ill one night, she had no water because their well was dry. The girl took their water dipper and went along the dark path to the spring. On her way back, she met an old man.

"All the wells are dry," he said, "and I am dying of thirst."

The girl gave him the water and went back to the spring for more for her mother.

At home, she carried the dipper into the sick room.

"Oh, thank you, dear," her mother said. "Now I can go to sleep."

Suddenly an amazing thing happened. The dipper floated out of the window, high up into the sky, and became the constellation we call The Big Dipper. And it was all because of the little girl's kindness.

When the story was over, Louise and I walked out in the yard and looked up at the darkening sky. The Dipper would be out soon. Insects had already begun their nightly songs.

The duskiness of the evening was kind of magical, for I was still a part of the story, where Mamma's wonderful voice had taken me.

Ranger stood out in the yard watching us. Daddy had put him on a long rope so he could reach the water trough and get under the shed. Louise went over to him.

"All right," Mamma cautioned, "you can't tell about German shepherds." But her voice didn't sound mad, as it had earlier when Ranger first arrived. Did that mean she might let us keep him?

~6~
# A Summer Evening

Back in the kitchen Guy bagged his peanuts and lined them up in a slatted basket. Tomorrow he would sell them on the streets of Ridge Spring. He counted them aloud. "Twenty-two," he said with pride. "If I sell them two for a nickel, I'll make fifty-five cents."

The kerosene lamp shadowed the corners of the kitchen. The smell of it was strong until Mamma went over and turned down the wick.

We all began to settle down, finding things to entertain ourselves until bedtime. Nobody mentioned Ranger. Maybe the others felt as I did that it would start an argument and then we wouldn't get to keep him for sure.

Guy got out his bags of marbles. He was good at the game and had a big collection from his winnings. The little round glass balls rolled against each other on the floor, making clicking sounds, as he sorted out the ones he'd be willing to trade.

Mamma picked up her crocheting and sat at the kitchen table near the lamp. She was always making something. This time it was Sunday dresses for Louise and me. Every now and then she called one of us over to measure her stitches, sometimes having to unravel some thread. She never used a pattern.

Daddy took down his gray farm ledger from the top of the pie safe. He stepped to the stove, lifted one of the eyes, and trimmed a pencil with his pocket knife, letting the shavings fall into the dead ashes.

"Will you trim one for me, Daddy?" I asked. I loved sharpened pencils.

"Find you one," he said.

I looked at the pencil Louise was using to rub a penny under a piece of brown wrapping paper from the grocery store. Abraham Lincoln's silhouette was already showing through.

"You're not getting mine," she said without looking up.

When school started, we'd each have a pencil, but one was hard to come by in summer. I gave up my search and got the one from my Tampa Nugget cigar box Daddy had given me. I knew the eraser had been used up, even the part that squeezed up when I flattened the metal around it with a hammer. I envied the nice slip-on eraser on Daddy's pencil.

After my pencil was sharpened, I moved to the table close to Daddy and watched him write in his strong, firm hand. Guy and Louise had him put their names in school books; I would too when I started first grade.

I tried to copy the letters he was writing, but I kept making mistakes. I needed an eraser! Finally, I gave up on that and drew a love knot. I started with a cross made from two straight lines. Then I drew lines from each end of the cross that circled around. I kept drawing these circled lines until they formed what looked like a knot made with string. It took a long time. My hand started to cramp, but I kept going. I liked the way the finished love knot looked.

"Guy, how much longer do I have to listen to the noisy clicking of those marbles?" Mamma sounded annoyed.

"I've got to put them back in the bags," he answered.

"All right. Go ahead and get it over with." The globe on the lamp was beginning to get smoky. Mamma leaned over and adjusted the wick again.

Daddy got up from the table and put his ledger back in its place on top of the pie safe. He removed the cigar from the corner of his mouth. "I just hope there's gonna be a market for cotton. If this depression gets any worse, I don't know what people will do."

"At least we have plenty of food." Mamma did not look up from her crocheting, but I was grateful they were talking to each other again.

"It won't buy gas," Daddy said. "The way you run up and down the road it doesn't last long."

"Awh," Mamma shot back, "you've got to have something to fuss about." Then her voice seemed to pick up a bit of merriment. "You're still mad at me for having my hair cut all those years ago."

I didn't remember when Mamma had long hair. But I'd heard that she was one of the first women in our town to get the twenties "bob," and she'd surprised Daddy with it. She had kept the long dark switch of hair that was cut off and stored it in our trunk. Sometimes I played with it.

"If Oscar and Maggie hadn't spoiled you rotten," Daddy told her, "maybe you wouldn't always have to do what *you* want."

Mamma tucked the right side of her hair behind her ear. "I never needed anybody to make decisions for me, if that's what you mean. I still don't."

Guy crawled up from the floor, yawning. Then he said what he did almost every night, "Well, y'all can stay up all night if you want to, but I'm going to bed."

Guy's malaria gave him headaches, especially in summer, and Dr. Frontis had him take quinine. He usually got tired at night before Louise and I did.

As he left the room, Guy turned and called, "Don't forget to say your prayers."

After Louise and I got into bed, she whispered, "Scratch my back." Mamma didn't like us talking after we went to bed because sometimes we ended up fussing.

"Then will you scratch mine?" I whispered back.

"Come on," she urged, turning so I could get a good reach.

I sat up and gave her back a good scratching.

"Okay," I said, "do mine." I lay down and turned on my stomach.

Louise didn't move or make a sound.

"You promised." My voice sounded muffled against the sheet. "I'm telling if you don't."

"Tattletale," she mumbled in half sleep.

I was mad. Mamma passed our doorway, and the lamp she carried threw wavy light into our room. I started to call out to her, but then I remembered how she disliked tattletales.

I turned on my back and fixed my hands for my prayers.

*Now I lay me down to sleep.*
*I pray the Lord my soul to keep.*
*If I should die before I wake,*
*I pray the Lord my soul to take.*

Then I added what I always said: "God bless Mamma and Daddy, Guy, and Louise, and," the most important part, "help Mamma and Daddy love each other." That night I added, "and let us keep Ranger."

# ~7~
# Ridge Spring

We were at the breakfast table when Pete called to Mamma from the back porch.

"Miss Grace? It's all right I git de slop?"

Twice a day Pete came to our kitchen for the big galvanized bucket that held the *slop* for the hogs. Leftovers, milk, and dishwater went into the bucket. The hogs liked the liquid with the corn Pete put in their trough.

Mamma got up from the table. "You're early this morning, Pete," she said. "Had your breakfast?"

"No, ma'am, but I kin wait. De hogs act like dey can't de way dey rooting and carrying on."

While Pete talked, Mamma dipped steaming grits onto a plate and added fried ham and biscuits. "Here," she said. "The hogs can wait. You need food in your stomach for all the work you do around here."

"I do thank you, Miss Grace." He nodded his head and repeated, "I do thank you." He took the food out by the well and sat to eat. I didn't understand why Pete never sat down in our house or came into any room except the kitchen.

Daddy got up to go the cornfield where he and Pete would finish gathering the ears ready for pulling. Some of the corn would be ground for meal; the rest, stored in the barn corncrib, for feeding the animals.

"Better leave the dog tied up until he gets used to the place," Daddy said. "He might run off and get lost."

Guy went in the pantry for the milk bucket. It was his job to milk Bitterweed. Guy had named our cow after she ate yellow-flowered weeds that made her milk taste bitter.

Pete returned his plate. "That dog look like he could be mean," he said.

"That's what I told Grady," Mamma agreed. "But the dog may not be around long." All the while she was piling a plate of leftovers to send out to him. She had, I decided, cooked extra grits just for Ranger.

Guy came back from his milking all eager to get to town to sell his peanuts.

"Just hold your horses," Mamma told him. "I've got to strain this milk and get it in the ice box." She spread a clean, loosely woven cloth over the shallow, flat-bottomed pan and poured the warm milk through it. Later, when the cream had risen to the top, she would take the pan from the ice box and skim the cream off with a spoon. We would make butter with it or serve it just like it was over blackberries. Sometimes Mamma made whipped cream with a wire whisk. We ate that on chocolate cake.

When we finally set out for town, Guy sat up front with Mamma. Louise and I bobbed up and down in the back as the Model A chugged up the slope and jolted us along the rutted country road.

"It's a good thing this car started," Mamma said. "I keep telling your daddy to park it on the hill so it can roll down and catch up, but he won't listen."

After a half mile of winding through cornfields, we turned onto the highway by the Ridge Spring town limit sign. Across the road from the sign was the town cemetery.

For the next half mile, except for an occasional house, the road was bordered by fields. Main Street, which was actually the highway, was the only paved road in our town of three or four hundred people, white and colored.

The colored people, as African-Americans were called in those days, lived in their own section of town, apart from the whites. They had their own separate school, church, and cemetery. Some coloreds, like Pete, lived in tenant houses on farms outside of town.

Stores lined both sides of Main Street, with a house or two sandwiched in between. On the right side, going into town, was a feed store, a drugstore that served "dope," as Coca-Cola was called, and a dry goods store. Dr. Byrd, the dentist, had his office over the drugstore.

Farther up on the right was a filling station, and beyond that the Baptist Church. In the churchyard was the parsonage and our school, with all eleven grades.

On the other side of the highway was the depot. Southern Railway passenger trains brought and took away our mail. Freight trains shipped our asparagus, peaches, and cotton to market.

On this day, few cars were parked along the street. Outside the post office men stood in a little group talking. At the filling station a car horn honked for the owner to come out and pump gas, wash the windshield, or check the engine's oil. Somewhere on a side road a car backfired. I jumped.

"Park the car, Mamma," Guy said. "There's Old Man Lige. He always buys peanuts."

Guy didn't mean any disrespect by using the term "old man." That was the way people spoke of older men in our town. It was a way of distinguishing a man from his son, who often had the same first name.

Mamma pulled in front of the granite bank building, and Guy hopped out.

Old Man Lige had a big potbelly and he waddled along with his walking cane. Seeing Mamma in the car, he touched the brim of his hat with his forefinger as a way of greeting.

As he poked along toward Guy, Old Man Lige reached into his pocket for change. "One bag still three cents?" he called out in a rusty voice.

"Yessir," Guy answered, "or two for five."

Old Man Lige stopped, looked down at the change in his hand, and brought up the other hand holding the cane to move the change around. "I don't want but one," he said, "and alls the pennies I got is two."

Guy handed him a bag, pocketed the two cents, said "Thank you," and went on down the street calling out, "Peanuts! Peanuts for sale! Two bags for a nickel!"

"That old tightwad," Mamma said under her breath as she opened the car door. "Louise, you go in the post office and ask if there's any mail for Grady Fallaw. Idella, you go to the grocery store and have them cut us a pound slice of cheese and grind a pound of coffee. Ask them to put it on our bill."

Louise headed for the post office, but I didn't move a muscle. I didn't want to do it. I knew farmers paid their grocery bills when they sold crops, and that was all right. I just didn't like to go in stores without Mamma.

"Well, go ahead," Mamma urged. "I'm going to the dry goods store to get some crochet thread."

"Can I say 'Mamma said'?" I asked.

"Yes," Mamma answered with a laugh, "you can say 'Mamma said.'"

Inside the store the smell of onions and kerosene greeted me. Two men sat on nail kegs with a checkerboard on a small table between them.

On the floor by the red-faced man was a can of kerosene. A raw Irish potato served as a stopper. "They ain't no jobs," I heard him say. "Looks like the govment's gone have to do something."

I went up to the familiar man behind the counter and told him what Mamma said she wanted. I waited by the barrels of sugar and flour while he stepped over to the cheese hoop to cut a wedge. The man who had been talking about "the govment" looked up from his game and asked, "Who's your daddy?"

Before I could answer, the grocer said, "She's Grady's baby girl. Looks like him, don't she?"

"Shore does." The man laughed before he added, "He's a good looker all right."

I felt my face flush. I didn't know why he had laughed. I watched the grocer weigh the cheese, wrap it in brown paper from a long roll, and tie the package with string pulled from a black holder. Then he ground the coffee beans, filling the store with the smell of Mamma's perking coffee. He poured the ground coffee in a brown bag and tied a string around that too.

"Your brother and sister with you?" he asked.

I nodded, and he reached into the glass case and handed me three jawbreakers: a blue, a green, and a red.

With a "Thank you" I hurried out, put the coffee and cheese in the car, and went up the street to find Mamma. The jawbreakers were getting sticky in my hand. I popped the blue one in my mouth.

I could hear Mamma laughing and talking before I opened the door of the dry goods store. Louise stood by a counter of boys' pants, and I walked toward her with my hand held open. She took the green jawbreaker.

"There's that other pretty little girl with long curls." I looked up to see a lady with big teeth standing nearby. "You don't need two little girls," she said. "You could give me one."

I edged up to Mamma and did my best to put my arms around her leg without opening the hand with the jawbreaker.

"Del–l—" My arm was cupping Mamma's dress between her legs and she gave me a gentle push. I held on. I didn't think she would let this lady have me, but I wasn't going to take any chances. There was no way I was letting go until I got out of the store.

Within arm's reach, brightly colored embroidery thread lay in little trays. I wanted Mamma to buy some, but I couldn't get her attention. She was trying—while I still held on to her leg—to show the lady with big teeth how to make a double crochet stitch.

After what seemed like forever, Guy walked into the store with his empty peanut basket. When he came near me,

I held open my hand. My palm was red. Guy took the jaw-breaker, popped it into his mouth, and walked around the store jingling the change in his pocket. I knew he wouldn't buy anything. He always saved his money.

Finally, Mamma stopped talking and we headed for the car.

Back at home, Mamma parked on the slope by the side of the house. Guy, Louise, and I jumped out and dashed around back to Ranger.

Louise saw him first. "Oh, no!" she hollered. "He's killed a chicken!"

# ~8~
# Gypsy Years

"A chicken killer!" Mamma stood over the dead chicken flung against the woodpile. Feathers lay scattered. "I'll bet you a pretty penny that's why that man gave the dog to your daddy. You can't break them."

Ranger did not get up to greet us. Instead, he lay on his paws, looking guilty.

"The chicken should've gotten out of his way," Guy said. "Ranger's tied up."

"I guess it would have if he'd known he was in danger. None of the other dogs we've had bothered them." Mamma picked up the dead chicken by its legs, walked over to Ranger and held it in his face. "Bad dog!" she scolded. "Bad dog!"

Ranger raised up, tucked his tail, and slunk backwards.

"Make his rope shorter so he can't get to the chickens," Louise offered.

"We're not having any dog around here that has to stay tied up." I could tell Mamma was still mad about Daddy bringing him home. She reached down and unfastened the leash. "If he gets another chicken, he's going right back where he came from."

Ranger took off running in circles around the yard. Chickens prancing about didn't know what to make of him. They high stepped it out of his way, spread their wings, and fluffed up their feathers. Several of them squawked.

We didn't know what to make of him either. Then Guy called out, "Come on, boy, let's go to the peanut field." Ranger loped after him.

I watched them go. I didn't want Daddy to take him back. I looked toward Louise to see if she might be feeling what I was, but she was already busy smoothing chicken scratches from the ground to draw a hopscotch. With a stick she drew blocks to hop in, making double ones in the middle and at the end where both feet would land.

We each found a piece of broken glass to jump over. Louise took first turn. She tossed her glass and jumped over it on one foot. At the middle and end she slapped down both feet, flipped around, and returned without a mistake. A game without an error gave her a second round. I waited my turn.

Victorious again, she said, "You can have it all to yourself. I'm going to find Ranger."

Wobbling on one foot, I started off. I was glad Louise hadn't stayed to watch me. Finally I gave up and went inside with Mamma.

I could hear her singing her favorite hymn, "In the Garden," above the clacking of the sewing machine. When I reached her, I saw she was making underpants for Louise and me from bleached flour sacks. Mamma never made our outside clothes from the bags. I was glad of that. Some children still had the faint letters from Adluh Flour on their shirts.

"Can I have the scraps?" I asked, and without waiting for her answer, went for my doll. I would make her some underpants too.

I spread the coarse cloth on the floor and laid my doll on it to measure her size, making sure I left extra cloth for seams and a hem on the legs. I also allowed extra to turn down at the waist.

"Could I have some elastic?"

"If I have any left."

"Could I borrow your scissors?"

Mamma handed them over, with "I knew that was coming."

While we sewed, I begged Mamma to tell me about when I was born. She knew I wanted to hear it exactly as she always told it.

She pursed her lips and began: "You were born in a little brown house in town on the same day as five little puppies."

"Why don't we live in that house now?" I asked.

"Because your daddy worked for the Highway Department, and he wanted us to travel with him."

"Tell me about the whooping cough."

"Oh, that was before our gypsy life. You were only one when you had that, and bronchial pneumonia. You had to learn to walk all over again."

"Why do you call it a gypsy life?"

"Because gypsies don't really have a home. They move

about and sometimes live in tents." She started her pedal going and raised her voice so I could hear. "The men on your daddy's crew lived in tents, but we had a kind of house fixed up from a big truck."

"We have a home now."

"Yes, we do, and we are mighty lucky to own a farm during this depression. We have our own vegetables, milk, and butter and raise our meat." Mamma held up her sewing and looked closely at the stitches.

"What's depression?"

"Hard times. People out of work. Nobody with much money. Some people will even lose their homes." Mamma looked unhappy as she talked about the depression.

"Why did we stop being gypsies?"

"Oh, we needed to settle down and start Guy in school. He was already seven."

Then as if she was talking to herself, Mamma said, "I can't believe I cooked for all those men on that work crew. And I didn't know *pea turkey* about cooking when I got married." She laughed out loud. Then her voice grew quiet and she spoke more slowly like she sometimes did when she was telling a sad story. "In the evenings we sat around the campfire and sang. One of the men played a harmonica."

"That's like Guy's mouth organ?"

Mamma nodded and started singing one of her gypsy songs. Her voice was mellow.

*It's only a shanty in old shanty town;*
*The roof is so ragged it touches the ground.*
*But my tumbledown shack by an old railroad track*
*Like a millionaire's mansion is calling me back.*

*I'd give up a palace if I were a king.*
*It's more than a palace; it's my everything.*
*There's a queen waiting there with a silvery crown*
*In a shanty in old shanty town.*

I tried hard to remember the gypsy years. Mamma's stories made it sound like she and Daddy were happy then. I did remember Daddy carrying me home half asleep one night from a silent movie with its tinny-sounding piano music. I imagined I could still feel the warmth of his shoulder.

And the hobo? Did I really remember seeing that tramp come to our campsite when the men were gone and Mamma ordering him away, holding a gun aimed at his back as he walked off? Or had hearing about it etched it in my memory?

I was about to ask Mamma to tell me more when I saw her wipe her eyes. She sat very still. Then in a husky voice she said, "I sure wasn't cut out to be a farmer's wife—not any more than your daddy was to be a farmer."

I was confused. Mamma loved our farm. She always took us on walks and picnics in the woods. Sometimes we went to the pasture stream and brought back violets to plant in our yard. She liked collecting mica from the hillside. We put pieces of it over the holes of empty thread spools and looked through to a golden world.

Why, I wondered, was she sad? I wanted Mamma to be happy.

## ~9~
# Ice Cream Day

The threat of losing Ranger hung over us. Chickens clucked and scratched about, but Ranger made no effort to chase them. That was a good sign. This particular morning he lay watching Guy whittle a whistle from a bamboo cane.

"If you cut your finger with that pocket knife," Mamma told him, "don't come crying to me." She had just gathered eggs from the hen house and had them cupped in her apron.

Louise sat on her tree saddle. Every now and then she looked down over the yard and shouted, "High ho, Silver!"

When Mamma passed by, Louise reined in her horse and called out, "You promised we'd go to town for ice to make ice cream. I wish we'd hurry up."

"Awh, if wishes were horses, beggars might ride." Mamma flung the words over her shoulder and disappeared into the house.

"That means you're a beggar, Louise," Guy taunted. "You're riding a horse."

"That's not what it means, Dummy." She made a move like she was going to climb down and fight about it.

"If you fuss," I warned them, "Mamma won't let us make ice cream." Mamma didn't have any patience when we argued. And she always carried out her threats. I thought of the day she threw our checkerboard in the fire because Guy and Louise kept fussing over their game.

Before long, Mamma called and we all piled into the car.

We were barely up the hill when Guy hollered, "Ranger's following us!"

Mamma slammed on brakes, pitching us forward, and jumped out. "Get!" she yelled. "Go back!"

Ranger stopped running and stood stock still. Mamma shouted again and again, but he just stood there. Outdone, she plopped back in the car. Working both feet frantically, she revved the motor, pumping the accelerator hard, and sent us scooting off in a cloud of dust.

When our trail cleared, we could see Ranger barreling after us. At the paved road, Mamma stopped the car. "That fool dog will get run over on this highway."

In moments Ranger was beside us, panting like crazy, his tongue lolling.

We sat waiting for Mamma to decide what to do when all of a sudden Ranger hopped up on the running board on Guy's side. In a flash he worked himself between the fender and hood and crouched down.

Mamma started up the car.

"Wait!" I cried out. "He'll fall off."

"Oh, no, he won't," Mamma said with all confidence. "He's found his niche."

The car pulled off, and we rode along, watching in disbelief as Ranger lifted his head to the wind. When Mamma parked the car in town and sent Guy in the store for rock salt, Ranger never left his spot. Colored people, already crowding the streets for their Saturday night get-together, cleared a space around our car.

At the ice house one worker called to another. "Come out here and look at this dog."

With our block of ice wedged in the back bumper,

Mamma turned down the street to our cousin Clyde, Jr.'s. She hadn't mentioned she was going to see if he and Aunt Ruby wanted to go home with us. I liked Clyde, Jr. He played with me. He would even play dolls.

Aunt Ruby didn't have to think about it. They hopped right in. "I never saw the likes of that dog," she said. "When did you get him?"

Her question got Mamma started. From "Grady just up and brought him home," she moved on to the chicken-killing story, and then just complained about Daddy in general. It lasted all the way home. Mamma didn't mince words when she started in on Daddy. I looked out the window at the shimmering patterns the summer heat formed in the air above the wheat fields and tried not to listen. I didn't like to hear Mamma talk about Daddy.

At home, Mamma said, "Guy, you get a croker bag for the ice. Louise, get the big dishpan hanging under the shed. The two of you can work the ice into it and bring it to the back porch."

Clyde, Jr., and I followed our mothers into the kitchen where Mamma set about making the vanilla custard. When we had company, Mamma laughed and talked. She did that now as Aunt Ruby sat at the kitchen table watching her. Mamma never measured when she cooked. She didn't even have any recipe books. She just put in a handful of this or a pinch of that.

"Dell," Mamma said, "you and Noonie"—as she called Clyde, Jr.—"get the churn out of the pantry and put it on the porch." She had started a fire in the stove to cook the custard. As she stood over the hot pot stirring, tendrils of wet hair stuck on her forehead and cheeks. "And, tell Guy we'll need another croker bag for the top of the churn."

In the yard Ranger lay on his side near my playhouse tree, his legs stretched out like he was still tired from his chase after the car. Clyde, Jr., drew back.

"He won't bother you," I said, and for the first time I went up and patted his head. He lifted it slightly and licked my hand. I knew then I could never, never let him go.

Guy was back at his whittling. "You get the bag," he told me. "It's in the back of the wagon shed."

I made Clyde, Jr., carry it. I didn't like the musty smell of dried peas that had been in it. Besides, it was scratchy.

Clyde, Jr., and I fidgeted about in the kitchen waiting for the custard to cool. It had to, Mamma said, or the ice cream would harden too soon around the edges and the dasher wouldn't turn.

"Go play horseshoes," Mamma said, "and forget about it for a while."

We reluctantly went outside, but we had no interest in the game of horseshoes, or in anything else for that matter, except bowls of frothy vanilla ice cream melting in our mouths.

Finally, Mamma brought out the custard-filled metal cylinder and locked it into place with the crank top and handle. She filled the space around the cylinder with chipped ice, stopping now and then to sprinkle in the rock salt.

I got to crank first and then Clyde, Jr.—since we were the youngest and the handle would get harder to turn as the custard froze into ice cream. When the churn began to *dance* with the cranking of the handle, Clyde, Jr., and I took turns sitting on top of the croker bag to hold it steady. The coarse burlap scratched my legs, and the sack's musty smell stuffed my nose.

As the ice melted, Mamma leaned the churn to the side and let water pour out of a little hole into the pan beneath it. Then she added more ice and salt.

When the crank wouldn't budge another inch, Mamma opened the churn.

"Can I lick the dasher?" Louise begged. "Can I?"

"No, you can't," Guy responded. "We all get to taste."

"Not this time." Mamma was emphatic. "I'm going to hurry and scrape it right back in so it can start to set good and hard."

Our mouths watered as we watched her run the big spoon down the sides of the wooden dasher to loosen the ice cream. Then she covered it up tight again.

"Go play," she said. "It needs to be real hard to dip."

"Let's find out who our sweetheart is," Guy suggested. He put a piece of ice and some rock salt in his hand. We knew his sweetheart was Mabel, a girl in his class. In first grade he asked Mamma if she could live with us when they got married.

Clutching the ice, he raced around the house. We waited to see the letter it would form on his palm—the one that would be first in his girlfriend's name. Back and out of breath, he wouldn't let us look. "Take my word for it," he said. "It's an *M*."

Louise called out the names of the worst people she could think of when Clyde, Jr., and I came back from our runs. Our voices had gotten loud by the time Mamma called, "The ice cream's ready!"

We held our crockery bowls and jiggled around the churn while Mamma scooped up mounds of cold, white ice cream.

Clyde, Jr., was the first to spoon in a mouthful. A look of surprise came over his face. Guy stopped the second spoonful on its way up. Louise ran to the screened door and spit.

Mamma jumped up and dashed to the kitchen. In seconds she was back at the porch door holding a bottle of dark liquid. My heart sank. It was Syrup of Figs, the nasty medicine she gave us for a laxative. She let out a rip-roaring laugh.

I knew what had happened, but it wasn't funny. The bottle Mamma held always sat in the cabinet next to the vanilla flavoring. Talking away, she had reached for the wrong bottle and poured.

Clyde, Jr., was the last to give up trying to eat it. Finally, he let his spoon fall back into the creamy dessert. "What made you do it, Aunt Grace?" he moaned, as his eyes filled with tears.

Even Mamma looked glum as she pulled the container from the slushy ice, marched to the kitchen, and scraped it into the hogs' bucket.

When she returned, her face was brighter. "Who wants to go to Old Shoals?"

Mine and Louise's answer was to dash to our bedroom and wriggle into our scratchy wool bathing suits. I loved the shoals where icy water rushed over large flat rocks, spilling into wading areas and ending in a deep, dark green basin.

At the sound of the car starting up, Ranger loped over and secured his spot. In a short while we were winding our way into the wooded area to join the few others already at the shoals.

The roar of the rushing water closed in about us, creating a different world. I tried my best to let the sparkling spray wash away the disappointment of the failed ice cream.

## ~10~
# The Punishment

The sound of the car cranking up continued to signal Ranger to his spot between the fender and hood. During the trips to town, he never once left his place. People in Ridge Spring grew accustomed to seeing the big dog riding on our car, but nobody dared come too close.

Workers who helped harvest our crops were glad when we took him with us. They were afraid of his fierce bark when they came to the well for water.

"Call the dog!" one of them would yell before daring to put a foot in the yard.

Trouble came on a Wednesday. That was the afternoon Mamma got her hair fixed in the Batesburg beauty parlor nine miles away. She paid one dollar for a shampoo and set while we went next door to the picture show for ten cents each. Sometimes we saw a western movie with Gene Autry, Tom Mix, or Roy Rogers. My favorites featured Shirley Temple. But today's movie was *Little Lord Fauntleroy* with Roddy McDowell. Guy and Louise weren't too happy about that. We had heard that the boy in the movie, Cedric, wore shirts with ruffled collars and acted sissy.

"Guy," Mamma said as we got ready to leave for Batesburg, "your daddy's not here to watch out for Ranger with the workers and we can't let him go. See if you can get him to the barn and shut him up in one of the stalls."

Guy coaxed, begged, and yanked to no avail. Ranger

knew something was up. Finally, Louise called out "Race you to the barn, Ranger!" and started running. Before Ranger knew what was happening, he was in the horse stall with the wooden bar pulled into place.

The picture show always ran a serial after the main feature was over. That day it was Flash Gordon. We gripped our seats in the darkened theater as Flash fought desperately to keep spacemen from invading our country. In the fight Flash Gordon faced mortal danger. Iron stakes were bearing down on top of him. Suddenly "To be continued" appeared on the screen. How could I possibly wait a whole week to find out if he was killed?

When we returned home in late afternoon, Ranger lay by the well. He had jumped the partition in the stall. Telltale feathers dotted the yard.

"Oh, no!" Mamma stood over a dead chicken. "That's one of my laying hens."

At the supper table nobody seemed hungry even though Mamma had fried pork chops and made rice and gravy. "We'll have to get rid of him," she told Daddy.

"Whoever you give him to will shoot him." Guy's voice was pitched high with worry. "That's what people do to chicken killers."

"Ranger won't have to be shot, will he, Daddy?" Louise asked.

Guy jumped up and left the table. I started to cry.

Daddy's jaws always popped when he chewed, but suddenly the room grew quiet. He said nothing, but drank the rest of his water, then pushed his chair back from the table. "I don't know of but one thing that might help." He turned toward Mamma. "Keep the children in the house," he said.

Mamma told Louise and me to go to our room and play. We found Guy there, standing by the window. We crossed the room and stood beside him, looking out across the backyard. We saw Daddy tie Ranger to the shed. Then he went over and picked up the dead hen. With a piece of rope he fastened the chicken's feet together and hung the carcass around Ranger's neck.

Daddy ducked into the shed and came out carrying one of the dogwood yard brooms. I heard a funny little squeal come up from my throat before it started to close up. I knew what was going to happen. Still, I could not make myself move away from the window.

Daddy lifted the broom and brought it down over Ranger's back. Ranger yelped and slunk close to the ground. Again and again he struck Ranger. The sharp yelps filled my head and I started to choke on my sobs. Pulling away, I ran to Mamma.

Back in the kitchen, after it was over, Louise was determined to go to Ranger. Daddy, breathing hard from the ordeal, put out his hand to stop her. "Not yet. He has to be left alone long enough to learn his lesson."

Louise looked at Mamma, but for once she was on Daddy's side. "You heard what your daddy said. You want to keep him, don't you?"

"You can pet him in the morning when I take the chicken off his neck," Daddy told Louise.

That night was one of the longest of my life. Louise tossed and turned beside me, and once I saw her shadow on the wall as she got up to look out the window.

When morning finally came, we saw Ranger loose in the yard, the chicken gone from his neck. We ran to him and showered him with kisses. He licked our faces in return.

# ~11~
# Grandma's House

I leaned on the edge of Grandma's long dining room table and watched her spread a newspaper dress pattern on pink-flowered material. She smoothed the paper out and laid silver kitchen knives to hold it in place.

Mamma had left us at Grandma's while she went to a meeting at the church. Daddy always complained that she was there every time the doors opened. I guess it did seem that way.

I loved being at Grandma's. The house smelled so fresh and clean. White organdy curtains with ruffled tie-backs hung at windows. Grandma's dress and apron always had a starched smell. Even when she was at home she wore silk stockings and a corset, a long close-fitting undergarment kept stiff with whalebone stays. Mamma had a corset too, but she wore hers only on Sundays to church and other special occasions.

My first name, Elizabeth, came from this grandmother. Her full name was Ida Elizabeth Hare Fallaw. "Idella" came from my maternal grandmother, who died before I was born.

"Idella—" Grandma's voice pulled me away from my daydreams. "Go check on Rob. I keep telling him he's going to keel over working in the garden in this heat."

I was glad Grandma didn't call her husband "Mr. Fallaw" the way her sister, Aunt Rhiny, did. Aunt Rhiny even called her husband "Mr. Cumbee" when she spoke to him.

Mamma said it was because she knew him when he was married to his first wife who had died. I was taught to use Miss, Mr., or Mrs. before all adults' names. Not even adults called one another by first name unless invited to do so.

From Grandma's kitchen I went onto the screened porch that circled around the back of the house. At the far end of the porch was a well. I tried not to look in that direction. Something about that deep, dark circle of water being near a bedroom gave me an eerie feeling. I hurried on out into the yard, squinting against the bright sunlight.

I could hear Louise and Guy playing with other neighborhood children on the railroad track in front of the house. They liked to get under the trestle, which was down a way, when they heard the rumbling of an oncoming train. I did it only once. That night I could still hear the roar of the train, smell the tarry cinders, and feel the ground trembling.

When I reached the hydrangea bush, I could see Granddaddy. His lean, slightly stooped body moved stiff legged down the bean rows. With a hoe he chopped at weeds. Waves of white heat shimmered up around him.

He caught sight of me, turned the other way, and spit tobacco juice. I thought about the time Daddy took him for a ride when our Model A was new. Granddaddy spit out the front window, and tobacco juice came in the back window on me. He would probably have strings of tobacco caught in his heavy mustache now, but I loved him anyway.

"Hey, Shingy," he called, using his pet name for me. Daddy's family did not give hugs, but I knew Granddaddy was always glad to see me. I could see his eyes smiling beneath his bushy eyebrows.

"Grandma said for you to come out of the heat." I looked

up at him, and the glare of the sun all but closed my eyes.

He leaned on the hoe handle and wiped his forehead on his shirt sleeve. "Tell her as soon as I finish getting the weeds out of this bean row."

A jangle from a horse-drawn wagon caught our attention. The iceman rounded the corner.

"And tell Ida to get a pitcher of ice water ready," Granddaddy added.

I knew Grandma's ice card on the back screened door would be turned to the number of pounds she wanted. I struck out in a run. I didn't want Guy or Louise to beat me to it.

The wagon creaked to a stop in front of the house. Careful to keep my distance from the old horse with his black blinders, I called out, "Grandma wants twenty-five pounds!"

"Awright, Little Missie." The iceman climbed down from the wagon seat and flashed me a big, white-toothed grin. "I thank you."

His smelly horse chewed at a metal bit, blubbered, and drooled a greenish fluid. Then he shook all over, scaring away flies and jangling his traces.

In minutes Louise, Guy, and two other boys huddled around the wagon. The iceman was still grinning as he stepped over his board seat and onto the bed of the wagon. He flung back burlap bags, uncovering big hunks of ice. With his ice pick, he made a straight line across a large block. Sparkling slivers bounced. We squealed, grabbing at the spraying pieces and sucking them into nothingness. The iceman laughed, lifted black tongs, and made them bite into Grandma's hunk of ice. It cracked away with a splitting sound. His arm muscles bulged as he lifted the block and stepped off the back of the wagon.

"Get you some chips," he said over his shoulder. "Den cover up de ice whiles I put dis in your grandma's box."

Everybody but me bounded onto the wagon and scrounged for ice. I wanted to in the worst way, but . . . *what if the horse decided to take off without a driver?*

Louise dropped a piece of ice down a boy's shirt, and a tussle began. I was glad when I saw the iceman rounding the corner of the house.

"Sit on the back ifen it ain't too wet," he called. "I'll ride you up the street."

Guy made room for me between him and the side of the wagon. Water trickled down the backs of my legs. It was cold!

The man popped the traces, the wagon creaked, and the horse's hoofs *clop-clopped* on the hard clay road. All too soon our ride was over. Somebody yelled, "Let's go to the tool shed!"

I liked the railroad tool shed. And the steep bank beside it was great for sliding. Once my friend Frances cut her leg on a piece of tin we used as a sled. It was the job of Frances's father to keep the rails repaired. Sometimes he let us ride the little cart he pumped up and down the rails.

I saw Grandma and Granddaddy sitting on the front porch, so I headed toward them.

A big pitcher of ice water sat on the banister. Grandma saw me coming and reached from the swing to pour me a glass. Granddaddy rocked in one of the big old green rockers with its flowered cushion. I climbed up in the swing next to Grandma.

We sipped water with ice tinkling in our glasses, and I told them about Ranger's punishment. "We left him tied up today," I said, "to keep him from following the car. But he can still grab a chicken if one comes close."

Granddaddy wasn't much of a talker, but I guess he could see I was worried. "I've heard tell," he said, "if anything'll break 'em, it's tying that chicken around their neck and a good whipping."

I sat swinging my legs back and forth while Grandma gave us a gentle push now and then. I thought about summer evenings on their porch. Sometimes after supper Daddy left us at Grandma's while he went to the poolroom. While we children played in the yard, the grown-ups talked. I liked searching for make-believe elves that lived along the railroad tracks. As long as the daylight held out, we raced around looking for footprints and other signs of elves or gnomes.

Later, when we came to the porch, I settled on Mamma's lap and listened to the talking. The songs of cicadas and frogs in the warm summer night provided background music. I drifted in and out of sleep until Daddy came to take us home.

Sitting there now with Grandma and Granddaddy, remembering the good times, I was happy.

# ~12~
# Ridge Spring Baptist Church

*Into my heart, into my heart,*
*Come into my heart, Lord Jesus.*
*Come in today. Come in to stay.*
*Come into my heart, Lord Jesus.*

I sat with my Sunday school class in a circle of little chairs. With our eyes closed, we sang the words ever so softly. I imagined if we were still and quiet enough, we could feel Jesus come. Miss Elizabeth, our teacher, sat on one of the low chairs too, the skirt of her flowered silk dress folded and tucked behind her legs where they bent at the knees.

After we sang, she told us stories from the Bible. Mamma had read us the same stories from *First Steps for Little Feet*. We didn't have many books, but of those we had that was my favorite. On the cover, flowers budded from a vine. Under the vine, a mother read to her little girl. When Mamma read, I was that girl on the cover.

I especially liked the story about Hagar being sent away with her little son Ishmael. I felt sad when Ishmael became sick in the desert and his mother could not find water for him. Because she could not bear to see her child suffer, she laid him under a low bush in the shade and stepped away to cry. It was then an angel from heaven came down and showed Hagar where to find water. After that, Ishmael got well and strong and grew up to hunt in the wilderness with a bow and arrow.

Guy always wanted to hear the one about the shepherd boy David who killed the giant Goliath. He liked the part where David hurled a rock from the sling he used against wild animals trying to harm his sheep. His next favorite was Daniel being thrown into the lions' den.

Louise liked the story of Salome, a dancer who asked for the head of John the Baptist on a platter.

Our Sunbeam teacher, Miss Katie, told good stories too. Once she told us about a rich man who was very sick. "I will give you all the money I have if you will make me well," he told his doctor. But the doctor couldn't, and the man died. Miss Katie wanted us to know that good health and many other things are more valuable than money.

On Wednesday afternoons at Sunbeams we took turns pumping air into the little organ with its slanted, carpeted pedals while Miss Katie played. Everybody sang "Jesus Wants Me for a Sunbeam" except the pumper. That person had to work hard to keep air in the pipes so the music wouldn't die out.

Miss Katie sang alto in the church choir. When Uncle Oscar, the brother Mamma lived with when she was growing up, came to visit us, he and Miss Katie sang duets. Mamma sang alto too, but her voice was much softer and mellower than Miss Katie's. Mamma didn't sing in the choir though. She sat in the congregation with us children. Daddy was brought up a Methodist, but he didn't attend church anymore.

One Sunday in church I learned why Mamma wanted to sit with us.

Mamma never let us turn around and look behind us in church, and we couldn't whisper once the service started. But this particular Sunday had nothing to do with either of those rules.

In such a small town, everybody knew if we had a visitor. That Sunday a visiting lady with a big-brimmed hat and lots of lipstick sang a solo. She had memorized the words to "His Eye Is on the Sparrow" so she didn't have to worry about holding the hymnal. That left her hands free.

As the lady sang, she clasped her hands before her. When she came to the chorus, she raised her arms above her head. With her hands still clasped, she turned the palms out and up to the ceiling. In that pose, she sang the words "I know he watches me" at the top of her lungs.

Guy's cheeks puffed out. I knew he was trying to hold his laughter inside. He sneaked a glance at Louise and then at me. Mamma gave us all a hard stare. It was too late! Even if God had told me to be still and quiet, I couldn't have done it, especially knowing the chorus would be coming up again. My tickle box had turned over.

Starting with Guy, Mamma pinched each of us on the leg. It really hurt, but our need to giggle was stronger than the pain.

"I'm ashamed of all three of you," Mamma said as we piled into the car after the service, "acting so ugly in church." She fussed and fumed all the way home. Driving faster than usual, she bounced us over the bumpy roads harder than ever. With a quick angry look toward the backseat where Louise and I perched in our crocheted dresses, she said, "Just because you look pretty with your satin ribbons around your waist, don't think you are. You just remember, 'Pretty is as pretty does.'"

We had been taught to be reverent in church—even when we went up on weekdays with Mamma to teach her Royal Ambassadors, of which Guy was a member. We would never run or shout, even if we were the only people there. I guess that's why our cousin Lithco shocked us the day he went with us. Even more daring than Louise, he walked the balcony rails with his hands stretched out like a tightrope walker.

I enjoyed being in the church when Mamma went early to get ready to cook hot dogs and roast marshmallows for her "boys." Sometimes she played the piano, and I would stand in the choir and pretend I was the lady who sang "His Eye Is on the Sparrow." One day I even walked down into the waterless baptismal font. When I was twelve, I would confess my belief in eternal life and be immersed there.

In the balcony a big rope dangled. Louise wanted to grab it and ring the bell in the worst way, but that was one dare she wouldn't take.

"The janitor let me do it once," Guy bragged. "The rope lifted me off the floor."

I always looked forward to visits from missionaries. Each time I heard them tell of taking Jesus' love to foreign lands and singing "Jesus Loves Me" in strange languages, I would tell Mamma I was going to be a missionary.

On summer Sundays the heat almost suffocated us as there were no electric fans or air conditioners in church. Ladies in their hats and gloves fanned furiously with bamboo fans or the funeral parlor ones that stood in the hymnal racks. I tried to think of the picnics our church had at Old Shoals and the big tin tubs of lemonade with hunks of ice floating. Sometimes that helped.

As soon as church let out, adults congregated on the steps, where the air stirred, to talk. We children ran behind the building to the spring our town was named for and the lily-covered pond the water trickled into.

Somebody's mother would always call out, "Be careful! That water's over your head!"

One summer, before I started to school, that spring lost its joy for me. A nine-year-old girl who was visiting her grandmother drowned there. The girl had tried to reach her ball that had fallen into the water. After that, all I could think about when I went to the spring was a ball bobbing and a little girl groping for her life.

*Mamma's brothers and sisters. Two brothers already deceased. Mamma is holding doll; Aunt Frances is on her left. Uncle Oscar is in upper left corner. Aunt Alice is just below brother at top right.*

*Grandma Ida and Granddaddy Rob, Daddy's parents, taken at their home in Ridge Spring.*

*Daddy and Aunt Frances. Mamma met Daddy while he and Aunt Frances were "courting."*

*Aunt Frances and Mamma.*

*Mamma and Guy by tool shed in Ridge Spring (before Mamma's "bob").*

*Guy, Idella, and Louise during "gypsy" years.*

*Idella, Louise, and Guy (in front) with cousins. Taken in front of tool shed.*

# ~14~
# School

Guy, Louise, and I sat on the kitchen floor and traced our feet on brown grocery paper. Mamma would send our foot patterns with the catalog order she was getting ready for Sears, Roebuck, and Company. As always, she would ask for room-to-grow in our black leather hightops.

"I'm going to school too," I announced as I bent to move the pencil around my bare toes.

Guy gave me one of his "Yeah!" looks, and Louise said, "Mamma, tell Idella she's not old enough to go to school. She won't believe us."

"Next year." Mamma responded, concentrating on the order. "You'll go next year."

Guy would be in third grade; Louise, in second. I didn't see why I couldn't go to first. I had never been to any school but Sunday school, as kindergartens were unknown in the South in the 1930s. More than anything I wanted to go to school.

I jumped up and ran to get Louise's last year's *Hill Reader*. For weeks I had carried the gray book around, asking Mamma what the letters spelled. Families had to buy school books. This one had fifty-two cents printed on it. Each year the books got handed down from one child to the next.

I still had my mind set on going to school when the catalog order came in at the post office and the opening of school arrived.

Since we lived off the bus route, Mamma drove Guy and Louise to school. On the first day we loaded in the car with me still insisting that I was staying too. But when Guy and Louise hopped out and headed with the other children toward the little building that housed grades one through four, Mamma cut that short. She didn't even switch off the car. She just turned right around and brought me back home.

"But I want to go to school, Mamma," I begged through my tears. My new shoes clumped behind her every step. I cried after her as she collected lamps and took them to the kitchen table to trim wicks and fill bowls with kerosene. I pulled on her skirt as she washed the globes in the sudsy dishpan.

On into the morning I kept up a "Why can't I go, Mamma? I can read, so why can't I go?"

Mamma turned to the stove, lifted an eye with the holder, and threw in the old wick ends. "If I've told you one time, I've told you a hundred. You have to be six to start school. You won't be until December 2."

It wasn't fair. I got Louise's hand-me-down clothes. I hadn't always wanted them. But I had waited to claim the reader. I wanted to do homework at night at the table when Guy and Louise did theirs.

"MA–MA!"

Suddenly Mamma jerked her apron strings loose at her waist and yanked off the loop around her neck. With a quick move she captured the hair falling over her face and tucked it behind her ear. "You are driving me crazy!" she exclaimed. "Go get in the car. I'm taking you up to that school. Let Miss Grace tell you you'll have to wait until next year, and maybe you'll hush up."

I should have been happy, but somehow I wasn't. I felt strange and scared. Miss Grace, the first grade teacher, had taught Daddy. She and Mamma had the same first names, but they didn't seem alike in any other way. Mamma was short with a softness about her body. Miss Grace was tall and stick thin. Mamma talked a lot, and you could tell by the way she acted if she was happy or sad or—most especially—mad. But Miss Grace had a quiet way about her. I had seen her many times. You could never tell what she was thinking.

My mind whirled. What if she did let me stay? Mamma couldn't stay with me.

I could tell by the way Mamma plopped in the Model A that she was mad with me. She had parked the car on the hill by the side of the house. For the second time that morning, she released the emergency brake and let the car roll. This time she mashed the accelerator up and down like she was mad with it too. The car picked up speed and she steered it toward the front yard. The motor coughed and sputtered. With her right hand she pumped the throttle in and out until the car fired up. Then she whipped it around and headed back up the hill.

I held onto the reader, and we bumped over the narrow dirt road. For a wonder neither of us said a word. Mamma's mouth was set tight.

After the half mile on the winding road and another on the highway, we were right in the middle of Ridge Spring. We passed the stores—with only a car or two parked here and there in front—the post office, and the Baptist church and turned into the school yard.

In front of the little building Mamma cut off the car and got out. I followed, taking giant steps to keep up. The warmth of summer still hung on, and the morning was heating up. Still, I felt cold as I followed Mamma to Miss Grace's room just inside on the right.

When Miss Grace answered Mamma's knock and invited us in, I could see boys and girls in rows of desks. I pushed close to Mamma and sneaked looks. They had writing paper and fat pencils, but they all stopped what they were doing and stared at me. My face felt hot. I burrowed into the folds of Mamma's dress and peered out. My heart ached to sit in one of those desks and do schoolwork, but I was scared.

Mamma seemed happier now. When she finished talking, Miss Grace put her hands in the big pockets of the sweater she always wore and looked down at me. "Let her stay," she said in a quiet voice, "and we'll see how she does."

Mamma left, and Miss Grace showed me to a desk. *Wouldn't Guy and Louise be surprised when they found out I was in school too?*

Shortly after I got settled, somebody in the wide hallway jangled a hand bell. "All right," Miss Grace said, "it's time for big recess. Stand by your desks the way you did for little recess. Row one, march to the playground. Row two . . . ." Miss Grace continued calling us row by row until all students were headed out to the playground.

Outside, my classmates broke away from the line and raced across the school yard. I stood there squinting against the sunlight and tried to figure out where they were headed and what they were going to do.

Suddenly a fourth grade boy yelled, "Hey, let's get that little girl with the long black curls!"

Before I knew what was happening, big boys raced toward me. Holding hands, they made a circle around me. I burst into tears.

"Y'all leave her alone," a familiar voice said. "She's my little sister." It was Guy.

# ~15~
# School Days

The next day I found out where the girls went during recess—over by the tall hedge to play *house*. Marjorie, the biggest girl in our class, was the mamma. She let me be her baby who had just learned to walk. Frances, Margaret Ellen, and the others were her children too. And we were all bad. Our mamma screamed at us for not helping around the house. When she tried to spank us, we ran from her. She caught us and dragged us back over the dusty playground. I loved it.

In the classroom Miss Grace was so busy she must have forgotten I was in first grade on trial. She wrote words on the chalkboard for us to copy, read to us, and listened to the stories we made up. She walked up and down the rows of desks—all bolted to the floor—and admired the pictures we drew and colored. Since gnats were bad, she showed us how to fold a piece of paper into an accordion-like fan to keep them away from our faces. Otherwise, we would get sore eyes and have to miss school.

When P. W. kept getting out of his seat, she stretched crepe paper on the sides of his desk to remind him to stay seated.

After the weather turned cold and the janitor kept a fire going in the big potbellied stove, Miss Grace had to sweep up the black coal dust several times a day.

"Class," Miss Grace said one day, "Paul is going to have another baby come live at his home. I think it would be nice if we made it a quilt."

I couldn't wait to begin. I loved to sew. The next day Miss Grace brought each of us a square of white material. "Now draw a picture that would be nice on the baby's quilt," she said, "and then I will show you how to embroider along your pencil lines.

While we drew, Miss Grace cut the bright embroidery thread into short lengths and divided the skein so we would use two of the threads. "If you don't know how to knot the end of your thread," she said, "come stand by me, and I'll show you."

I knew how to roll the thread down my finger to make a knot so I began embroidering the house I had drawn with windows and a door and smoke curling out of the chimney. We didn't have embroidery hoops like ours at home so Miss Grace kept reminding, "Now, keep your cloth pulled tight across your left hand so the material won't bunch up." I made a chain stitch in a single line of black thread to outline the house. Then I did a satin stitch by putting gray threads close together for smoke from the chimney.

I looked forward to embroidering each day and dreaded the time when Miss Grace would say, "All right. We must put away our squares."

It took so long for some classmates, especially the boys, that I had extra time. I made green slashes of grass and drew trees to embroider the trunks brown and leaves green. With lazy daisy stitches, I put yellow flowers with brown French-knot centers.

One day while we worked on the quilt, Miss Grace looked deep in thought. "I don't know what we should do about Darling's square. Does anybody know why he hasn't been to school?"

I was curving black lines to make birds in my sky, the very last thing I could possibly do. Suddenly I had an idea.

"Miss Grace," I said, "my mamma saw Darling's mamma, and she said he wasn't coming back to school. Could I do his?"

She gave me one of those looks I mentioned when you don't know what she's thinking, but she didn't say a word. It made me feel kind of funny. I felt everybody looking at me.

I don't remember if Darling came back to school, but I do remember that I did not get to embroider his square.

When Miss Grace let me start first grade, Mamma bought me a Blue Horse tablet, a pencil box, crayons, and a small pair of scissors. Most of all, I loved the nice new crayons with their waxy smell. The ones we had in our tin box at home were all broken with paper peeling off. I had a burning desire to take my school crayons home overnight though I knew we weren't allowed. Then I had another idea.

"Miss Grace," I said, "Mamma wants to know if you would let her use my crayons today. She wants to color a picture."

She gave me one of her looks, then surprised me by saying, "We'll see."

She still had not mentioned the crayons when school was over. I was afraid to ask her again, the way I would Mamma, so I went out disappointed.

I was in the car with Mamma out by the flagpole waiting for Guy and Louise when I saw Miss Grace heading toward us. She held her hand across her forehead to shield her eyes against the sunlight. Like a jack rabbit I scrambled into the back seat and scrunched down in the floor.

Even with my head pressed hard against the back of the front seat, I could hear her telling Mamma about the fib I told. Mamma laughed her gusty laugh and said something I couldn't make out. When Miss Grace left the car, Mamma whipped around toward the back seat. "I *would* hide my face," she scolded. "You ought to be ashamed of yourself."

I was ashamed. Still, I couldn't understand why Miss Grace wouldn't believe me the day I told her I could sew on Mamma's Singer sewing machine.

"I know you can when you get a little older," she replied.

I thought about telling her what Mamma always said before I sewed. I would beg and beg until finally she would say, "All right, young lady, sew! But don't yell for me when you run that needle through your finger." I wondered though if this would be telling something I wasn't supposed to. I knew Mamma didn't really want me to hurt myself. Every morning when she dropped me off at school, she'd say, "Take up for yourself and don't be a tattletale."

After Guy rescued me from the bullies that first day of school, nothing bad enough ever happened to make me think I needed to take up for myself, and I tried not to tattle.

When I got home each day, the first thing I did was play with Ranger. Then I taught my imaginary students. Daddy had given me one of his big old gray ledgers with unused pages. I put my students' names in it and wrote down the grades they made. One day, I promised myself, I would be a teacher—just like Miss Grace.

# ~16~
# The Boatwrights

We had only one close neighbor, the Boatwright family. Even so, the slope of the land did not allow us to see their house or they ours. Mamma and Mrs. Boatwright, or Vila as Mamma called her, were good friends. They enjoyed exchanging cuttings from their porch plants.

"I would thank you," one of them would say, with a hint of laughter over a superstitious belief, "but if I did, my cutting may not live."

Sometimes when Mrs. Boatwright visited, Mamma forgot to send me away to play. Adults did not allow children to sit in on their conversations. But I would never leave unless Mamma told me to. I loved to listen to their talk, even if I didn't understand some of the things they said.

"I heard that straight from the horse's mouth," Mamma told her friend.

"Well, I wouldn't take a pretty for hearing it." Mrs. Boatwright seemed excited.

"The last time I saw her," Mamma went on, "she looked like 'Who-shot-Lizzie.'"

It never entered my mind to ask who looked like whatever that was. Children did not enter grownups' conversations unless they were asked a question. Besides, I pretended to be occupied with my doll so they'd forget I was close-by. Every now and then I sneaked glances.

Like Mamma, most of her friends wore sleeveless cotton

dresses in the summer heat. For some reason their slip straps kept falling over their upper arms. I thought it odd that the straps twisted into tight little rolls. Even washday did not unwind them. I took a special interest in how long the ladies would put up with the discomfort of the dangling strap before thrusting a hand in the neck of the cotton print dress and yanking it back into place.

One afternoon as they talked and laughed and pulled up slip straps, a loud thump startled Mrs. Boatwright.

"Oh, that's just Louise jumping out of a tree onto the roof," Mamma said. Then turning to me as if she saw me for the first time, she said, "Dell, go tell your sister I said get off the house before she breaks her neck. And stay outside and play."

On my way out Mamma said something in a low voice to Mrs. Boatwright who threw her hand up to her face and exclaimed, "Awh, hush your mouth!"

Was she really telling Mamma to keep quiet? I sifted her words in my thoughts and tucked them in a little niche of my mind. When I grew up, would I talk that way?

The Boatwrights' two younger children were near in age to Louise and me. They sometimes rode to school with us. P. W. was in my class. Kathleen was what people of the time called "afflicted." She walked in a jerky way, often falling and keeping her knees covered with scabs. Once she fell into their fireplace and suffered bad burns. She was a sweet, quiet girl with a pleasant expression, and everybody was nice to her.

"I'll tell you one thing," Mamma often said after Mrs. Boatwright's visit, "that Vila is one smart lady." She'd cluck her tongue and add, "Now you can put that in your pipe and smoke it."

At play I pulled Mamma's and Mrs. Boatwright's expressions from the niches of my mind, rolled them around on my tongue, and repeated them to my imaginary friends. It didn't matter that I did not have the slightest idea of their meaning.

# ~17~
# State Fair

Summer was slipping away. September tinged poplar and sweet gum leaves with yellow and red. We couldn't wait for apples to ripen on our tree on the slope. Louise climbed up and threw some down. Then she hung by her knees from a lower branch. In her offhand way Mamma warned, "Green apples give stomach aches." We ate them anyway and suffered through gripping pains and a healthy dose of Syrup of Figs.

Workers came to the farm to pick the white fluffs of cotton spilling from prickly bolls. Fear of Ranger's bark and bristling fur showed in their faces. He had become protective of his family. We kept him inside when workers picked in fields near the house.

I looked forward to the coming of the pickers with their burlap bags carried by a sling over their shoulders. I wanted to be out there with them. Guy got to as long as he didn't miss school, but Daddy would never let Louise and me.

"The cotton field's no place for little girls," Daddy said when I begged. "Besides, the monkey might get you."

I knew he meant the sun would be too hot for us, but some children in my class got to. They even missed school. And the colored children picked. It wasn't fair.

I had to content myself with sitting on the furrows and watching and listening. I liked to hear their back and forth good-natured joking.

Each of the workers had his own style of picking. Some crawled on their knees, wearing holes in their overalls; others bent over rows. Most worked two to a row, a picker on either side. That way they didn't have to reach over and risk ripping a finger on a sharp burr. A few of the older workers had all but the tips of their fingers wrapped in rags to protect their hands.

When their bags were full, pickers dumped the cotton on burlap sheets at the end of the rows. Except for a few workers who prided themselves on how much cotton they could pick in a day, most families put their cotton together.

When the sun sat low in the sky, Daddy rang the big bell in the yard to call the pickers in. This was the best time of all. The strong oily smell of cotton seeds mingled with that of burlap as workers gathered under the big oak to have their day's pick weighed. With the corners of the sheets tied together, Pete helped Daddy heave the bundles up to the scale hook.

"Dat's my own!" somebody called out, and Daddy came back with "Two hundred pounds!" Shouts went up as Daddy recorded the amount in his ledger.

All was quiet while the next sheet steadied itself on the scale. "Two hundred seventy-five!" Daddy yelled out.

A tall, slender picker slapped his leg. "I knowed I could do it!" he exclaimed. "I knowed I could."

Even Pete, who was usually solemn, smiled to see the happiness.

With the weighing over and the workers gone, we let Ranger out. He romped with us while Pete and Daddy loaded the cotton onto the wagon under the shed. Later Pete would take the load to the gin to be baled—that is, pressed tight and bound with metal strips. Afterwards it would be brought back to the farm until there was enough for shipping. I liked playing on the big bales. I pretended I was on a stage telling stories to my audience who was made up of chickens pecking around the yard.

It was the sale of cotton that made it possible for us to have money for the state fair in South Carolina's capital city, Columbia.

Great surges of joy flowed through me for weeks before the fair. I could smell the pungent aroma of hot dogs and taste the sugar of cotton candy. The sound of barkers trying to lure people to the tent and *toss* shows rippled through my head. I could feel the anticipation in Guy and Louise too.

"All right," Mamma warned, "you better not act ornery if you want to go to the fair. None of that bickering."

At last the day arrived. We rarely went anywhere as a family, but Daddy went with us to the fair. Sounds and smells greeted us at the crowded gates. Balloons bobbed above the heads of clowns flopping around on big feet. Shrieks shattered the air near the roller coaster.

"I want to ride the merry-go-round," I begged. "Let's go there first."

"No, the ferris wheel," Louise said.

"Just hold your horses," Mamma told us. "Let me get my bearing."

To our surprise, Daddy said, "I'm taking Guy," and they disappeared through the crowd.

I could tell Mamma didn't like that one bit. She grabbed each of us by the hand and marched toward the merry-go-round. Its spellbinding music was like a fairy godmother beckoning. Soon I was a princess riding my horse in a magic kingdom. I wanted to ride it again and again, but Louise kept begging for the ferris wheel.

I was afraid of the ferris wheel, but, since it was so rare for Louise to want to do anything with me, I let her talk me into riding. My stomach felt hollow as the loud-talking man fastened the bar across our seat and pulled a lever, making us rise. Just as suddenly as we'd risen, we stopped. The seat rocked furiously. He stopped us again and again to let others on. Each time we dangled higher and higher until we reached the tip-top. I had never been so high.

"Gosh!" Louise peered over the side. "Look how short the people are." I got up my nerve and looked. They did look small, like ants working their way in and out of games and shows. I couldn't find Mamma, but I could see the top of the merry-go-round swirling round and round.

We started to move again. Each time we scaled the top and started down, hanging with nothing beneath us but the ground, I left my stomach behind. People around us screamed—some in fear, others in delight. I clutched the bar. Louise grinned from ear to ear. Time after time we were swept up and over the top. Finally, the great wheel stopped turning and we got off. I wobbled toward Mamma on Jell-O legs. I was proud of myself, but I didn't want to ride again.

Next we went to a tent show where trick dogs wore funny little outfits. A blonde lady in a fancy red dress smiled and waved a wand while dogs walked on hind legs and jumped through hoops. Midway the show a clown sold boxes of Cracker Jacks. Each of our boxes had a tin popper inside. When the popper was pressed, it sounded like a cricket chirping.

As always we saw the *midget* show. The sweet faces of the little people smiled down from the stage as they danced and sang. In a different show a man swallowed fire, and in another a man rode a motorcycle on the sides of a giant tub buried in the ground. I wondered if Guy would see that.

With the smell of food all around us, we ate hot dogs, candied apples, and strips of sugary bread. Louise and I had orange slushes. Mamma was happy to find iced tea.

"I don't want to miss the steel building," Mamma said, pulling us in that direction. She enjoyed seeing the canned vegetables and baked goods. Both of us liked the handmade afghans and embroidery, but Louise was eager to see the animals. I liked the little yellow biddies, but the smell of the stock barns was ten times stronger than our barn.

After the two of us giggled ourselves silly trying to find our way out of the crazy house with its mirrors, Louise begged for the freak show. Mamma didn't like us to go there, but she finally gave in. One lady was so fat she couldn't get up from her chair by herself. A man had six toes on each foot. When we passed the jar with tiny Siamese twins in it, Mamma said, "That's enough. Come on."

Finally, stuffed with cotton candy and too tired to walk another step, we went to the gate to wait for Guy and Daddy. We had not caught sight of them all day, though I could tell Mamma kept watching.

All the benches were full, and there was no place to sit. A loud speaker kept repeating, "So-and-so, meet your family at the gate." We wanted Mamma to have Daddy called but she wouldn't. She got madder and madder as we waited. "He had no business running off with Guy that way," she fumed.

I heard the speaker say, "We have a little blonde-headed

boy wearing a green jacket. If he belongs to you, please claim him." I looked up at Mamma.

She sensed my concern. "There's no way either of you could have gotten lost," she said. "You've hung on to me the whole day."

Evening air nipped at us and crowds made their way out the gate when Guy and Daddy finally appeared.

"It's about time!" Mamma quipped and struck out walking toward the exit gate.

In the car she lost no time in giving Daddy a piece of her mind. "I know you took Guy places he had no business," she accused.

I didn't understand what Mamma meant. We had seen the freak show—at least part of it. At first Daddy tried to laugh it off without denying whatever charge it was Mamma was making. But, as usual, Mamma's anger was contagious and Daddy began to fight back. After a hot exchange of accusations, we rode home in silence.

At bedtime Mamma brought out what we dreaded: Calomel. Through the years we'd been told the little pink pill would keep us from getting *bilious* from all the junk we had eaten at the fair. How could the stomachache from the junk be worse than the one Calomel would give? I wondered. Too tired to fight, we gave in. Besides, Mamma had been known to hold medicine in one hand and a switch in the other. Regardless, I already looked forward to the fair next year.

# ~18~
# Butchering

When frost formed a crystalline coating over the land, talk among the grown-ups turned to butchering. From this time throughout the winter months, cured meat could hang in the smokehouse without spoiling. That was important since ice boxes did a poor job of keeping foods, even for short periods. Freezing was not an option.

From the time I heard Daddy tell Pete to round up *help* for butchering on Saturday, I felt anxious. I liked having the happy workers in our backyard. They knew a share of the meat and, more importantly, the *chitlins* would go home with them. But I felt sorry for the hog. I didn't want to see him slaughtered, even though I knew he was raised to feed our family.

On Saturday morning I bundled up against the brittle air and followed Louise out to the long wooden tables set up for butchering. The help had gathered, and their jolly talk filled the air. Flames curled from underneath two big black washpots, and scalding water sent up steaming whirls. Louise went over and stood by the pots. She didn't want to miss a thing.

I edged over to my pretend house under the oak. Still, I could not get away from the grinding sound of knives being sharpened on the great whetstone by the shed. Guy turned the handle while workers pressed long-blade knives against the stone's roughness until the cutting edge glistened in the thin sunlight.

Suddenly the sound I dreaded most—a high-pitched squeal—split the air. Two big men struggled to pull the hog to the assigned spot. I tried not to look as one of them grabbed the hog's snout and thrust his head back. Squeals became muffled grunts. In a motion as quick as a striking snake, the other man slashed the hog's throat. Blood gushed. My head swam.

Men stood ready with buckets of water. They splashed it on the spurting blood, washing the hog's body down and turning the ground the color of rust. Someone slit the tendons of the hog's hind legs and fastened hooks from a wagon singletree behind its hamstrings. A worker grabbed the rope dangling from the singletree and threw it over an oak limb. With much heaving the men hoisted the hog's body off the ground, feet first, with the rope. After it was tied in place, the body was once again doused, this time with scalding water from the black pots.

When the repeated scaldings had softened the hide, workers eased the body down and gathered around to remove the coarse hair on the animal's skin. With great force they scraped until the skin glistened white.

Louise stood close, taking it all in. I wanted to go inside and get away from what I knew was coming, but I would be alone there with my thoughts. Mamma was busy telling the women which part they must be ready to receive in their white enamel dishpans.

Without meaning to, I looked just as a knife slit the hog open. Insides tumbled out. Pans accepted the liver, intestines, and other parts. With the intestines spread on a worktable, women's hands turned them inside out, cleaned, and washed them. These would be used as casings for sausage.

The well chain creaked as the pulley brought up bucket after bucket of water. One of the men cut the hog into parts: hams to be cured by salting and later smoking, great hunks of fat to boil in the washpot for making lard, ribs for barbecuing, loin for cutting pork chops, and side meat for bacon.

At another table, workers fed the cut-up shoulders and other leftover meat into a metal grinder fastened to the side of the table. This ground meat would become sausage. With hot pepper and other seasonings added, the meat was fed back through the grinder. This time a woman held an intestine stretched over the opening. The meat wound out, filling the casing. The process was repeated until all the meat was used up.

Fires blazed under the black pots again, this time to make lard. All but a small amount would be stored in tin pails for use in making bread and frying. The remainder would be the main ingredient in strong lye soap. Bits of skin and meat from the bottom of the pot would be saved to make crackling cornbread.

Nothing was wasted. The liver and jowl, the hog's cheek, went into another pot for making liver pudding.

Pete gathered hickory wood and built a slow fire on the ground inside the smokehouse. Men carried salted hams, side meat, and sausage links and hung them from the rafters. The process of curing the meat had begun. The fire would be kept up night and day, and by Thanksgiving smoke from the fire would flavor and dry the meat. More importantly, the curing preserved it for use throughout the year.

The hard work was over. Tired but happy workers lugged home pans of meat, including the hog's feet and head that would be pickled or used to make souse, sometimes called hog head cheese.

I was glad butchering was done for another year, but I looked forward to Monday. By the time I got home from school, Fanny would be through with the washing and ready to make lye soap. I would watch her.

For supper that night Mamma cooked sausage and grits. I thought about the hog, and I couldn't eat the sausage.

# ~19~
# Making Soap

During school Monday, I thought about Fanny. She would be making soap when I got home from school. I remembered the time I went to her little house, between where we lived and town. She was making a hoecake for her husband, None. She mixed flour and lard in a bowl, like I had seen Mamma do, and added milk a little at a time. I noticed how smooth and light the palms of her hands were as she floured her enamel-topped table and turned the stiff ball of dough onto it. With her hands dusted in flour, she patted the dough into a circle the size of the greased skillet heating on the iron stove.

None, a big man, sat at the other end of the table rolling his cigarettes in thin little rectangular sheets of white store-bought paper. With one hand he held the paper. With the other he tipped his drawstring tobacco sack. The strong-smelling tobacco fell into the bend he made in the paper. Then he licked the gluey edge and rolled it into a cylinder. It was the first time I had ever seen a man make his own cigarettes. No women I knew smoked except an aunt by marriage who was from the North.

The hoecake bubbled, and Fanny lifted the edge with a knife to see if it was ready to turn. After a couple peeks, she flipped the hoecake over, turning the browned side up. When the second side browned, she took the hoecake up, poured homemade sugarcane syrup on it, and set the plate before None. I thought he would pull up closer to the table to eat. Then I noticed his stomach was so big he couldn't get any nearer.

When school was out that day and we got home, I dashed out back where Fanny smiled at me across the washpot. "You just in time," she said. "I'm 'bout to put de lye in. But you stand back now. This stuff eat your eyes out."

I knew that Fanny had made the lye by soaking hardwood ashes. After the soaking, she boiled them. Flames licked up around the washpot where she had melted lard saved from the butchering. Now she sprinkled the lye onto the fat and stirred the mixture until it came to a boil again.

I moved as close to the washpot fire as I dared so I could feel its warmth. As Fanny stirred, I asked, "Why didn't you bring your grandbaby today?"

"Her mamma she come down and tuk her back to Chicargo."

"Why did she do that?"

"Her mamma got married." She smiled. "And I happy 'bout dat." She turned the corners of her mouth down. "But I show does miss dat sweet little thing."

I was confused. I thought you had to get married *before* you could get a baby. I started to ask Fanny, but I thought better of it.

Ranger had gotten over his excitement of having us come in from school. He lay near my playhouse, now littered with fall leaves, and watched with sleepy eyes. He liked Fanny. I guess he knew she would never bother our family but had come to help us.

Occasionally Fanny stopped stirring to poke the fire back under the pot and add wood, or to test the boiling liquid in a bowl of cold water she had nearby. If she didn't cook the mixture long enough, it wouldn't harden. Then it couldn't be cut into bars.

Mamma liked the way Fanny made soap. "Some cook it too long," I'd heard her say. "That turns it brown. Fanny's white soap doesn't have that strong odor either."

We used Fanny's lye soap for washing clothes and scrubbing floors. In the kitchen we used orange-colored Octogan soap bought at the store. Each time I opened a bar, I counted its eight little flat edges that gave it the name.

Finally the part I liked best was ready. "Go tell your Mamma to get de cloth. We ready to strain it."

Mamma kept old muslin curtains for making soap. She brought out a panel and spread it over a little wooden box that looked like a small horse trough. With me holding one end to keep it in place and her the other, Fanny dipped the hot liquid with a white enamel dipper and poured it into the mold.

"You do make as pretty a soap as I've ever seen, Fanny," Mamma complimented her.

"Yes, ma'am, lot of folks after me to make dere soap."

I had been so interested in watching Fanny I hadn't given a thought to what Guy and Louise were doing. Now I saw them down at the barn where Pete stood in the back of the wagon pitching out corn stalks. He would stack the stalks on end, leaning them against each other to make a fodder shock. In this shape the leaves and stalks would dry for barn animals' food.

"Dell," Mamma said, "go tell Guy and Weezie not to be playing on the fodder shock. It'll have them all scratched up."

I ran off to deliver the message, but I knew once Pete stacked the fodder like an upside-down top, the temptation to climb up and slide down would be too great, even for me.

Already I could hear Mamma's voice when we took our baths, "If you'd listened, you wouldn't be so miserable now."

# ~20~
# Country Winter

Cool breezes whooshed down our slope and we could almost taste the nip in the air. The last of the mellow gold leaves dropped and bare trees showed ragged clusters of sticks on branches where squirrels nested. Migrating birds fluttered against the horizon and settled in the tawny yellow of wheat stubble left from the fall harvest. We no longer sat under the walnut tree cracking the thick-hulled nuts and eating the meat. But, like squirrels, we gathered and stored them away.

Guy helped Daddy and Pete dig sweet potatoes. Louise and I played at raking rust-colored leaves with Mamma and Floride. Suddenly Louise dropped her rake and jumped headlong into the crunchy lightness of a big mound. I did the same.

"All right," Mamma said, "stop scattering the leaves and

get back. I'm ready to burn them."

She struck a match on the side of the little wooden box and held it to the pile. The leaves sparked, flamed, and flared into the sky, then fell back into the flickering flames. When the dance of leaves waned, Mamma pushed at them with her rake and sent them whirling again.

The tangy smell of smoke reminded me that cold days were coming. I hated to give up playing outdoors and sitting on our porches. Instead we'd hover around the kitchen stove or fireplace.

"Look!" Louise's shout broke into my thoughts. She raced one way and then the other about the fire. "Smoke follows beauty!" she giggled. "Everywhere I go it follows me."

Mimicking her, I flirted with the smoke, trying to make it follow me. Mamma and Floride laughed at our silliness.

When the sounds of the wagon caught our attention, Louise headed toward it and the earth mound behind the woodpile where Daddy and Guy would bury sweet potatoes to protect them from frostbite during winter.

I went inside to watch Mamma and Floride make sauerkraut. A light frost had readied the cabbage heads. Now, quick hands pulled leaves from the thick stalks, and washed and chopped them to fine shreds. Next, they packed the shredded cabbage into a big brown jug to ferment in a brine made of salt and cabbage juice. I wouldn't eat kraut because I didn't like the way it smelled, but the rest of the family liked it with sausage on cold days.

When they had stored the kraut in the pantry, Mamma paid Floride for her help. With a "Thank you," Floride reached inside the neck of her dress and unpinned a handkerchief. She untied a knotted corner and added the money Mamma gave her to the change already there. Then she pinned the handkerchief back inside her dress.

Like every farm wife, Mamma took pride in her pantry and invited guests to see jars filled with okra, corn and tomatoes, pole beans, beets, and squash. Peach and pear halves swam in their juice, and pickled peaches with cloves stood ready for Thanksgiving and Christmas. Jellies and jams from blackberries and wild plums, along with preserves from peaches and pears, were there, ready to sweeten buttered homemade biscuits. Dried peas and beans sat beside the flour in small wooden barrels. If visitors did not have a garden, Mamma pulled down jars for them to take home.

At first frost Mamma insisted we put on our winter undershirts—our BVDs. Louise and I also donned thick black stockings that came up above our knees and under the hems of our dresses. We rolled the stocking tops over bands of elastic to keep them up.

Sometimes an elastic would come unstitched. When that happened, we pulled the top of the stocking out to the side, twisted it into a tight lump, tucked it in, and rolled the stocking down over it. With much activity, it came loose and had to be twisted and tucked again.

Life on the farm came almost to a standstill at this time of year. One winter, a neighbor, who had the misfortune of a possum falling in his well, came to get water from ours. "If I knew who left the cover up on that well," he said, "I'd take a stick to him."

Twice a day Pete came up to the house for the slop. Each time the door opened, icy wind whipped in. Always, air pushed down the hill behind our house.

"We're paying for the nice breezes we got this summer,"

Daddy said.

At night, wind howled under the house like it was searching for something. Now and then it stopped for breath. Then it would start up again.

Mornings, it was hard to crawl from beneath our heavy quilts and pull on cold clothes. Still, school was my bright spot on winter days that chapped hands and faces. Classmates who waited in the cold for school buses had cracks in their skin. Some even had bleeding lips.

Afternoons, back at home after school, Mamma let me stand on a chair and wash dishes or play with leftover dough that I shaped and reshaped into cookies for my doll.

Sometimes I stood at a window, misted it with my breath, and wrote the words I'd learned to spell.

Louise and I folded brown grocery paper the way Mamma had shown us and cut out paper dolls that held hands. We drew different expressions on their faces and colored their clothes. I put mine in a circle and let them play Drop the Handkerchief.

Sometimes we children made belts by folding paper and fastening the pieces together in tight joints. Other times we made pinwheels by bending corners of paper squares and sticking a straight pin through each into the rubber eraser on a pencil. When we blew on our pinwheels, "Mine goes faster than yours" usually led to an argument.

If Daddy was home, he'd say, "Grace, come in here and see about these kids." He depended on Mamma's "Do you see the fire in my eyes?" look to set us straight.

After disciplining us, Mamma's mood often changed as quickly as a chameleon's color. She read to us from *Grimms Fairy Tales* or told stories about when she was in school. We laughed each time she told about the teacher who kept calling her down for talking. "Grace," her teacher asked, "why don't you just come up here and teach the class?"

Some nights we made butter. Mamma put the cream she saved in the butter churn and let it sit on the hearth to warm up so the butter would form more quickly. Whichever of us was through with homework could churn. Some folks had churns that looked like the jar Mamma packed sauerkraut in. That kind had a wooden top with a hole for a dasher that plunged up and down. But ours was glass with a metal top and a handle like our ice cream churn. I liked it because I could see the cream sloshing as we turned the handle.

As we churned, little yellow specks formed in the milk. Every so often Mamma checked to see if the butter was ready. She always took the last turn because she could tell exactly when the yellow pieces should be removed.

When it was just right, she poured off the thickened milk, called buttermilk, and put that aside to keep for drinking or making biscuits. Then taking the little yellow blobs of butter in her hands she worked them together into a ball, squeezing all the milk out. Next, she pressed the ball of butter into our wooden butter mold, which had a rose pattern carved in the bottom. When Mamma turned the mold over and pushed the butter out, the rose lay on top.

Ranger shared our evenings before the fire. I laid my head on him and dreamed. Now and then I fell asleep. I was always surprised when Ranger woke me beating his tail on the floor.

We didn't buy ice during winter. The unheated pantry kept foods cold. Grandma had a little screened area outside a kitchen window where she kept her milk and butter.

The worse part of winter was my bouts with tonsillitis. Antibiotics had not been discovered, but Mamma had her own remedy. For croup, she gave me a teaspoon of sugar with a few drops of kerosene sprinkled on it.

At bedtime, she sat me on her lap before the fire and rubbed my throat and chest with Vicks salve mixed with turpentine. The odor took my breath away. I could never decide which was worse—the smell or the heavy sticky feeling. My protests of "MA—MA—" did no good. To make matters worse, she warmed a piece of white flannel from an old nightgown and pinned it under my pajama shirt. The smell of turpentine seemed to stay with me for days.

The few times the homemade remedy didn't work, Mamma took me to Dr. Frontis, my teacher's father. He sat on a little stool in front of me and said, "Stick out your tongue." When I opened my mouth, he whipped out a long cotton swab from behind his back and mopped my tonsils with Mercurochrome, a red medicine we used for scrapes and scratches.

Even worse, he said, "Keep her home from school for a few days."

We didn't need excuses from home when we were absent from school. Miss Grace lived with her parents and Dr. Frontis would tell her I was sick, or she would ask Guy or Louise about me.

During those days at home, I pined away wishing I could be at school. The only time I didn't mind missing was when Mamma held a quilting bee.

With the big frame set up before the fire, Mamma and her friends stretched quilt tops across it. They spent the day talking, laughing, and quilting patterns like "wedding ring" or "Jacob's ladder."

Underneath the frame I pieced together a quilt for my doll. I was a mother too. From my *pretend* world, I caught snatches of the ladies' conversations. In between talking about the neatness of their stitches, somebody said, "She's going to stir up a hornet's nest if you ask me."

"All I know about her," another chimed in, "is that she can talk the horns off a billy goat."

"Well," a high, thin voice said, "I wouldn't know her from Adam's house cat."

"He knows how to get her goat," Mamma said. "I'll say that."

I heard the word *pregnant*. Then somebody remembered I was under the quilt frame and whispered, "Little pitchers have big ears." But I didn't have to worry. Mamma wouldn't send me away from the fire even if I didn't have tonsillitis.

So I played on, listening to the words running back and forth between the ladies like their stitches.

# ~21~
# Christmas

Talk of Christmas began right after Thanksgiving. This year, though, many voices had lost their ring of happiness. The Great Depression, which had begun when I was four, grew increasingly worse. Clouds of debt hung over families. Tramps—or, hoboes, as they are sometimes called—were a common sight along the roads. Some rode freight trains. During long water stops at the depot, men came to Grandma's begging for food. She fed them.

"The axe is out by the woodpile," she would say. "You split some stovewood-size pieces while I fix you something to take along."

Mamma said, "Hoboes pass the word about which house to go to." I figured they had heard about the homemade biscuits Grandma kept in the pie safe. We grandchildren liked to poke holes in those biscuits with our fingers and pour syrup in them.

In spite of hard times, Mamma managed to keep her spirits up by staying on the go. Daddy said her middle name was "Go."

Each December she drove us to Columbia to see the Christmas lights in the stores and visit Aunt Maggie and Uncle Oscar in the house where she grew up.

As soon as school was out for the holidays, we took off. It didn't bother Mamma if the car sputtered and stopped. She pulled her coat tight around her, hopped out, and raised the hood. In minutes she was tapping a little thing called a carburetor upside down on the fender and replacing it under the hood.

Back in the car, she started up the motor. "Somebody gave your daddy gas with trash in it," she'd say.

We entertained ourselves along the forty-mile trip by watching for Burma Shave signs. I didn't need to know all the big words as Guy and Louise kept trying to beat the other one at reading the signs. "I proposed" one read, and on up the road another said "To Ida." Farther on came "Ida refused" and after another distance "I'da won"; still farther, "My Ida" and finally "If I'da used Burma Shave." We repeated the advertisement all together like a poem until we came to another.

Louise had memorized them all. She sang the words out even before we reached them, and Guy said, "Make her hush, Mamma." He liked "Every shaver . . . Now can snore . . . Six more minutes . . . Than before . . . By using Burma Shave."

Aunt Maggie was always glad to see us. She was a quiet, dignified lady who, according to Mamma, never quite knew what to do with her when she was growing up. This day she had bananas for a special surprise.

Uncle Oscar, who kept books for a lumber company, came home for dinner at noon. A tall, stout man, his dress suit was a firm fit. A gold chain ran across the front of his vest and disappeared into a small pocket. Now and then he drew out his gold watch, pressed a little button that flipped open the cover, and checked the time.

Before Uncle Oscar returned to work, he held out a balled fist to us children. "If you can  open my hand," he said, "you can have what's inside."

On my turn he teased by letting me lift one finger while keeping the others clamped tight. I couldn't help thinking how different his hands were from Daddy's. Uncle Oscar's looked as if he never did anything to get his dirty. Finally, I felt his strength give, and the promised nickel was mine.

After dinner, we went to a big store where Christmas music played and bells and wreaths hung from the ceiling. Great numbers of people moved all around us.

Near me a mother yanked her little son away from a water fountain. "Don't drink from that!" she scolded, dragging him to another fountain close-by.

I pulled at Mamma's dress. "Why can't he drink that water?" I asked.

She leaned down to my ear and cupped her hand over

her mouth. "The sign above it says 'Colored,'" she whispered.

I didn't understand. Did the colored people in Columbia have different water?

Suddenly bright lights shone down on the most toys I had ever seen. It was then my eyes rested on the doll. She had a mouth like a rosebud. Her lips were parted ever so slightly so she could be fed. Like my old doll, she didn't have hair, but wavy patterns molded to look like hair showed from under a pink organdy bonnet that matched her dress. More than anything I wanted to hold her, but I was too shy to ask.

Then I saw Mrs. Santa. She was dressed like Santa Claus, except she wore a dress. Her cheeks were rosy from living in cold weather.

"I'm sorry Santa couldn't be here today," she told us. "He had to go back to the North Pole to check on things."

To my surprise, she took the doll from the shelf. Holding it so I could see, she leaned it back. The doll's eyes closed! Mrs. Santa turned her over. The doll cried. Then, wonder of wonders, she placed the doll in my arms.

When Mamma said we had to go, I was still standing there holding the doll. All the way home I thought about her. She and my old doll would be friends. I would love them both. If only I could have her!

"Mamma," I begged, "I want that doll for Christmas."

"Well," she said, "we'll have to see."

Every time we talked about what Santa would bring us, Mamma would say, "Times are hard." Always, she added, "We're lucky to have a smokehouse full of meat, plenty of milk and eggs, and a pantry to carry us through the winter."

I knew Santa would bring new shoes. He always did, as we'd usually worn out our school ones by then. Besides, the old shoes were getting small. Our family never hung stockings, and we didn't exchange presents. I pictured Christmas morning. Under the tree would be two boxes for each of us kids. One box would hold our new shoes. The other box would hold clusters of raisins still attached to the stems, tangerines, a pencil, and a gum eraser.

I had seen children at school with cardboard inside the soles of their shoes. I was willing to do that instead of getting new shoes—if I could just have that doll. I told Mamma so.

I guess I pressed her too far one day.

"Oh, stop fretting," she snapped through pursed lips. "Santa may not make it at all this year."

I tried my best not to think about what Mamma had said!

Louise and I made paper chains for our cedar Christmas tree cut from the pasture. We colored strips of paper and glued ends together with paste made of flour and water. The chains looked pretty with the silver tinsel, which we saved from year to year. Nearer Christmas, Daddy and Guy would gather mistletoe.

Dusk came early, and in the long evenings Mamma read to us before the fire. We heard *The Night Before Christmas* so many times we had it memorized. While she read, I lay with my arm around Ranger and dreamed. Sometimes dreams of the doll made my stomach ache.

When Christmas Eve came at last, I curled under the heavy quilts and tried my best to go to sleep. I said my prayers and for the last time asked God to let me get the doll. I thought of Miss Katie at Sunbeams. "If you pray and believe," she said, "your prayers will be answered." Still, I knew my prayers had to end with "Thy will be done." Maybe for some reason God did not want me to have the doll.

At dawn I awoke with a start. The house was still. Somewhere a rooster crowed and dogs barked. My heart quivered. I slipped from under the covers to the icy floor and through Mamma and Daddy's room to the tree. *The doll leaned against the shoe box!* Without looking at anything else, I grabbed her up and held her close.

Standing quietly on Mamma's side of the bed, I patted her face to wake her and held up the doll. At first she looked confused. Then she nodded and smiled. "Go back to bed," she whispered, "until we get a fire going."

I took my doll to bed and watched her close her eyes in sleep until Daddy got up and started fires in the fireplace and the kitchen stove.

Guy got a BB gun. He was so happy he sat down and rocked it. Louise got a pair of boy's pants with big pockets— just what she wanted!

It was the best Christmas I ever had.

At Grandma's later in the day we gathered with our aunts and uncles and all of our many cousins. They came from Batesburg, Johnston, Wagener, Aiken, Sumter, and even as far away as Hamlet, North Carolina, where Uncle John, Daddy's brother, was Chief of Police.

Along with the wonderful smells of turkey, pan dressing, and all the trimmings, whoops of laughter filled the air.

"You stoutened up there," one adult told another. To the children it was, "My, you've grown a foot!"

Even with Grandma's long table, it took three seatings for everyone to eat. The youngest ate first. After we had our desserts of chocolate pie, Japanese fruitcake, and ambrosia, the teens took our places. Then came the grown-ups, who lingered longest at the table.

Aunt Josephine, Uncle John's wife, liked being with us children. She found some of us in the parlor where we sat telling what Santa Claus brought us. Carolyn, an only child, got the most. I thought it was strange that Santa would bring her more just because she didn't have any brothers and sisters.

Aunt Josephine, who wore her hair in a stylish pouf, played the piano for us. As we were taught to do in the presence of adults, we all sat quietly. It was unusual for an adult to take time with children unless they were teachers. Children were expected to entertain themselves.

Lithco, our daring cousin, must have thought Aunt Josephine was odd to want to be with us. "How old are you anyway?" he asked.

Aunt Josephine's hands froze on the piano keys. She turned toward him with pressed lips, which accentuated the little brown mole on the edge of her mouth. "Young man," she scolded, "you should never ask a lady her age."

Then she put her smile back on for the rest of us. "I want to hear what you're studying in school," she said.

When responses didn't come quickly, she raised her eyebrows. "You do like to study, don't you?"

"I like to read," Louise said.

"I'm so glad." Aunt Josephine smiled brightly. "I'm sure you do your studies too." Then with a broad sweeping gaze, which lingered on Lithco, she added, "I abhor laziness." She tensed her body and held her shoulders back. "Why, if I had a lazy bone in my body, I would go the doctor and have it removed."

Of all that happened at Grandma's that day, the thing that stuck in my mind was Aunt Josephine's lazy bone remark.

I gave it lots of thought. When I told Mamma, she threw back her head and laughed. "That sounds like Josephine," she said.

How, I wondered, would the doctor know where a person's lazy bone was? What if he removed the wrong one? From that day on, I vowed I would not be a lazy person just in case it was something doctors looked for.

# ~22~
# The Great Depression

On New Year's Day we had the traditional southern meal: black-eyed peas and collard greens. Eating peas assured we'd have change money—coins—during the coming year; greens, the *green*, or paper, money.

We children liked *hoppin' John*—peas cooked with rice—best. Hoppin' John must have some mystical power because it made us want to jump up and down. That was a happy time!

But for most people, 1932, the bleakest year of the Depression, was not a happy time. Many lost their jobs and could not make their rent or house payments. Some lost homes because they could not pay the taxes on them. Banks failed. Store owners who had allowed customers to buy on credit lost their businesses.

Though I had not seen them, I heard that hungry people stood in long lines waiting for free food from the government. Men were ashamed because they could not support their families. Some lost faith in themselves and in the future. A few even took their lives in despair. Songs were written about men jumping off bridges to their deaths.

In our town, churches and farm families helped the needy. Hardly a day passed that Mamma did not take chickens, eggs, milk, and butter to families in town. Some lived in large homes with beautiful furniture, but they had no money for food. On Sundays relatives flocked to our house for a good meal. Afterwards, Mamma loaded them up with food to take home.

Though we were fortunate to have food, we too had little money for items like kerosene for the lamps, black pepper, sugar, salt, and Mamma's coffee.

We were all in the kitchen after our New Year's dinner, Guy, Louise, and I still hopping from the rice and peas. Suddenly Guy stopped. He stood stock still, listening to something Daddy was saying to Mamma. Louise and I did the same.

"Looks like the only choice I've got"—Daddy took a cigar from his shirt pocket and rolled the tip of it in his mouth—"if we want to keep the farm."

"How do you know you can get your job back?" Mamma asked.

"I contacted Mr. Hook. He says he hasn't found a decent foreman since I left." Daddy drank the rest of his water and got up from the table.

"You're going back to work on the highway?" Guy asked in disbelief.

Daddy nodded. "We need the money," he said. "The cotton market was way off this year." He struck a match on the sole of his shoe and lit his cigar. "You'll be all right with Pete's help."

"I'll need the car," Mamma said.

Daddy nodded again and put on his hat.

My insides felt hollow. I sidled up to him, something I

rarely did. He put his arm around my shoulder and gave me a squeeze. "I'll come home when I'm close-by."

The next day when we came home from school, Daddy was gone. Mr. Hook had come for him. I missed him already—even his cigar smell.

Daddy's absence didn't seem to bother Mamma. Folks in town asked, "Grace, aren't you afraid to stay way out there by yourself?" Mamma would laugh and come back with "I'm not afraid of the devil himself."

One night not long after Daddy left, she had an opportunity to prove her courage. We heard strange sounds coming from the pasture bottom. It sounded like a man yelling in pain—then again, it could have been somebody singing. I was scared. We never locked our doors. Nobody we knew did. We didn't even have keys for our locks.

"Awh," Mamma comforted, "it's just some drunk trying to find his way home." She got out a book and read us the story of "Half-done Polly." We knew the story well. Mamma called Louise and me Half-done Polly when we started something we didn't finish, like the girl in the story.

With one ear I was listening to the story. With the other I was trying to make out the sound coming from the pasture. Now and then Mamma paused as if she was listening too. Then she'd start up again. Finally, Louise said, "Turn Ranger out and sic him on whoever that is."

"No!" Guy yelled. "They might shoot him."

Maybe what Guy said put an idea in Mamma's head. She hopped up and headed for her bedroom. In a flash she was back with a loaded shotgun.

"You going to shoot him?" Louise was excited.

"Heck, no," Mamma answered. "I'm just going to scare

the daylights out of him." She cupped a hand around the lamp globe and blew out the flame. The eerie glow from the fire cast shadows over our night clothes.

"Guy," Mamma ordered, "come over here and hold up this window."

While we all shivered from the cool night air, Mamma got down on one knee and placed the gun across the sill. Suddenly a blast like an explosion boomed into the night.

After that, the only sound we heard was Ranger's whine. The noise must have hurt his ears too.

The next morning when Pete came up to the house, he seemed eager to speak for a change. "I heard a gun go off las' night."

Mamma laughed. "Oh, that was me. I shot out the window to show some trespasser I meant business."

"Yes, ma'am," Pete said. "He sho know dat now. He sho do."

For days afterward my insides felt jumpy. I missed Daddy, and I didn't want a drunk man yelling in our pasture ever again. Back in the 1930s, nobody asked children about their feelings, and since I didn't know how to talk about them anyway, I just kept quiet. Then one evening as we sat around the fire, I burst into tears.

Mamma put down her crocheting and took me onto her lap. "What hurts?" she asked.

I shook my head.

"Then why are you crying?"

"I—I don't know," I sobbed.

"Well, I know one thing." She cuddled and rocked. "You're too little to be worried."

For a wonder Guy and Louise didn't say a word.

## ~23~
# Louise

A cold moon outlined leafless tree branches outside our bedroom window. Icy winds whistled and prowled beneath the house, causing the yellow bell bush to scrape against the windowpane.

I missed Louise. She was in Mamma's bed because she was sick. Her fever was high, and she talked *out of her head* in a wild, excited way.

"Don't let him get me!" she called out. "He's coming after me!"

I could hear Mamma soothing her, something she rarely needed to do for Louise. It was strange to see my sister like this. When I thought of her, I could see her arm wrestling with Guy or climbing trees. Like Mamma, she was strong-willed and independent. And she never got sick. I was scared.

"Mamma," I called in a soft voice. In seconds her shadow was in the doorway of our room. "My feet are cold."

She turned. Footsteps crossed the floor; then quiet. Her step again, the covers lifted, and a wool sweater warmed before the fire was tucked around my feet. With a pat on my leg through the quilts, she turned and went back to Lousie.

I tried hard to go to sleep, but the storybook sandman with his sleepy dust would not come. My body cramped, but I dared not move and touch cold places in the bed. I felt lonely and sad. I wished Daddy was home.

The rocker squeaked against the wood floor. I could not

remember Mamma ever rocking Louise. I lay listening to the wind and the sound of the rocker, drowned out now and then by Louise's *crazy* talk. I was sorry I had ever wished for a bed all to myself. What if Louise died?

I wanted to call out to Mamma again, but I knew I shouldn't. Louise needed her more.

Then Mamma started to sing. "Sweet hour of prayer, sweet hour of prayer, that calls me from a world of care . . . ."

On and on her rich voice strung words over the melody as easy as her stitches slipped over her crochet needle. I closed my eyes and let the sound lull me to sleep.

# ~24~
# Snake

Louise was better the next morning and refused to believe she carried on the way she did. In fact, she didn't even want to admit being ill. Mamma said Louise didn't have sore throats the way I did or headaches like Guy because she ate fruits and vegetables.

As the days went by, we continued to dress in the teeth-chattering chill of early morning and huddle around the fire in evenings. Finally, we made it through the winter months.

Daddy had not been able to get home, but an early spring lifted our spirits. After being cooped up all winter, we couldn't wait to get outdoors.

Once the fear of frost was over, Pete plowed and mounded the soil for planting sweet potato slips. Under rain and sun, green heart-shaped leaves pushed out like large fans along the vines.

I was glad Mamma wasn't particular about when we could go barefoot. Some mothers wouldn't let their children go without shoes or take off their BVDs until school was out no matter how hot the weather. But not Mamma.

Every day after school, I got out of my black leather high-topped shoes, peeled off my long stockings, and wriggled my toes in the cool spring earth.

For a wonder, we children were getting along as we romped with Ranger up and down the rows of the sweet potato field.

Many times we had heard Mamma boast she wasn't afraid of anything, but we knew better. She had a mortal fear of snakes. "If you'd been bitten by one like I was when I was little," she told us every spring, "you'd be scared of them too."

On this particular afternoon she was remaking ladies' dresses into church outfits for Louise and me. Daddy's sister, Elizabeth, had married a Yankee and moved north—something southerners didn't do often back then. "Sister," as she was called, had lots of pretty clothes and occasionally sent dresses she didn't wear anymore to Mamma to be "made over" to fit Lousie and me. Today, Louise would get the pongee one, as the light brown color would look good with her auburn hair. I would wear the white, lace-trimmed dress.

"Watch out for snakes!" Mamma yelled through an open window.

"Yeah," Guy cautioned, "watch out for snakes." There was too much fun in his voice to take him seriously.

"A snake bites the third person," Louise announced.

With that, she high stepped it over a broad-leafed plant and jumped in front of Guy, making him the third one.

Guy jumped back in front of her. I knew a fight was brewing. I was about to yell for Mamma when Guy let out a shriek that scared even Louise. She hadn't touched him yet.

"A snake!" he screamed and clutched his bare foot. "A snake bit me!"

He wasn't teasing. His cry sounded too real. He took off in a hobble toward the house. We ran too, yelling for Mamma. She met us on the front porch. Guy plopped down, holding his foot and moaning.

Mamma's face showed alarm as she bent over the two red marks on top of Guy's foot, which was already swelling.

"Louise," Mamma ordered. "Run get Pete. I'm going for the doctor."

When Mamma saw Pete coming, she hopped in the car, released the brake, and let it roll down the hill. The motor started. She whirled the car around and pressed the accelerator for all she was worth. I'd never seen Mamma fly up the road like that.

Pete stooped down by Guy. "Don't you worry none," he said. "I'll fix yo foot up." He pulled a wad of chewing tobacco from his mouth and plastered it over the snake bite. "Nawh, Suh. No need to worry none."

To my surprise, Guy stopped moaning. Pete took out a package of Brown Mule tobacco from his overalls pocket, pulled off another plug and started chewing. As soon as he had a new wad ready, he plastered it on and put another chunk in his mouth. Trails of brown juice ran down Guy's foot and onto the porch. The smell of tobacco grew stronger and stronger.

All the time Mamma was gone, Pete kept chewing and replacing the tobacco. "You gone be awright," he kept repeating. "Yes, siree, bob tail squirrel jenny. You gone be awright."

We were lucky to have two doctors in our town. Mamma moved lickety-split down the hill, with Dr. Brunson—who delivered me—hot on her trail.

With all of us bunched around, Dr. Brunson took a good look at Guy's foot. "Well, Guy," he said, looking up at Pete, "I believe you've already had the best doctoring you could get."

As he was told to do, Guy stayed off his foot until the swelling went down.

We never did find out whether the snake bit the second or the third person. When it struck, Guy and Louise were jumping around each other too much to tell. But we did learn Daddy was right: with Pete's help we would be just fine.

# ~25~
# Daddy

Guy had a money-making project for every season. In fall, it was capturing rabbits in homemade boxes hidden in broom sedge along the field furrows. When a cabbage leaf lured a rabbit inside the box, a trap door dropped down, taking him prisoner.

One afternoon I tagged along as Guy checked his boxes. "Hot diggety dog!" he exclaimed when he saw that the door to the third and last box was closed.

I stooped with him and peered inside. A frightened rabbit cowered in the back of the narrow box. Guy reached in, caught him by his front legs, and pulled him out. Keeping him in a firm hold, he marched the rabbit home to the prepared pen. His catch safe, Guy went in the house to tell Mamma.

I looked at the little rabbit cowering in the pen, his ears twitching in fear. With only a moment's thought, I turned the wooden latch. The wire door swung open. As quick as lightning, the rabbit scooted past me and ran for his life. He hopped again and again toward the field, his feet barely touching the ground.

I don't like to remember what followed. Mamma was as upset with me as Guy was. "What on earth possessed you to do such a thing?" she asked. "You know Guy sells the rabbits we don't eat."

Things might have been worse for me had it not been for the sound of a car. A man was bringing Daddy home. Ranger ran up to the car, barking and wagging his tail at the same time.

Just inside the front door, Daddy dropped his grip—as a suitcase was called—and gave us children quick hugs. He looked different. In place of his usual hat, he had on a cap. He was handsome in his long-sleeved white dress shirt and tie.

Mamma stood in the kitchen doorway speechless. She stepped back and let Daddy pass through.

All of a sudden Daddy pulled off his cap and cut a fancy dance step on the kitchen floor. He whirled around and grabbed Mamma by the waist.

Mamma was in no mood for dancing, though, and she jerked away, giving him one of those searing looks she used to discipline us children.

"Do you know how long it's been since we've heard from you?" she fired.

"You would have heard if I hadn't been all right," he answered, still grinning.

"But how did you know that *we* were all right?" she shot back.

Daddy looked thoughtful, and a little hurt. Then Louise said, "A snake bit Guy, but Pete put tobacco on it."

He faced Guy. "You all right?"

Guy nodded.

"Well, I'm home now." His grin came back, spreading across his face. "And tomorrow I'm having a horse and pony delivered." He looked at Guy. "The two of us are going to ride over this land."

"Me too," Louise hurried to say. "Can't I ride too?"

"Of all the—" Mamma didn't give time for a response to Louise's question. "You've got less sense than I gave you credit for if you've spent money on horses for pleasure. I thought you went back to the highway department so we could keep the farm."

After I went to bed that night, I heard them fussing. The next morning Daddy took us to school. Mamma had a sick headache. She had been up all night rubbing her forehead with Mentholatum.

True to Daddy's word, in the afternoon a slick brown horse and a Shetland pony arrived. Though Mamma was still angry—and we didn't like to do anything to make it worse—Guy could not conceal his happiness as he and Daddy saddled up. Louise rode too, but not me. Even with Daddy holding the reins, I was still too nervous.

While Mamma was in her garden, I hurried and climbed on a chair to wash the dishes. I loved to surprise her.

"Oh," she exclaimed coming through the doorway, "a

brownie has been here!"

I beamed.

"Dell, did you see a brownie while I was out?" She reached over and hugged me and smiled. I was glad she didn't have a headache anymore.

In the evening when I tucked my dolls in for the night, I lay thinking until I remembered a fishing trip our family took together. On the way to the river, Daddy let Guy sit on his lap and steer the car. At the water's edge we stepped out on flat rocks and threw our lines in. The whole day was filled with laughing and talking as we caught fish to fry. The scene was so clear in my mind, I imagined I could even smell the water that reminded me of wet logs. Lost in that happy memory, I drifted off to sleep.

# ~26~
# Aunt Betty

When Daddy's highway job took him away from home again—this time to Virginia—Mamma started "taking in" people.

First she took in a lady and her young son who had come from the North to live with her sister. The sisters had a falling out, and the mother and son stayed with us until she could arrange for money to return home.

After that, Mamma took in a girl who had a baby, "out of wedlock," as I'd heard it whispered. The girl's father had put her out of his house in disgrace. To my disappointment, I did not get to play with this baby the way I did Fanny's grand.

The mother picked it up only to nurse it and tucked it back in her big bed. I never heard it cry.

The person who stayed the longest was Aunt Betty. She wasn't kin. We called her "Aunt" out of respect for her age. Like the others, she helped about the house. Aunt Betty was a spinster—an "old maid." When I heard people use the term old maid, I thought of our card game, Old Maids. Nobody ever wanted to be *it*.

When I was little, girls were expected to marry by their early twenties. If they didn't, older married ladies looked at them sadly and clucked their tongues. "What a shame," they'd say. "The poor thing missed the boat."

Like many unmarried women of the time, Aunt Betty did not have a home of her own but moved around from relative to relative. When a family member had a baby or someone got sick, Aunt Betty moved in. Mamma heard at church that she now had nowhere to go since noboby in her family needed her. So, this tall, thin lady in her flour-sack dress, black stockings, and high-topped shoes came to live at our house.

Aunt Betty did the ironing. Though I was shy with most adults, I felt comfortable around her. I became her shadow when I wasn't in school.

Fanny still did the wash, but Aunt Betty took the clothes from the line. With a shawl wrapped around her knot of gray hair, she brought in pieces starched stiff as scarecrows. She sprinkled them down for ironing, and stuffed them in an asparagus crate until she was ready to iron. I watched her set up the ironing board across the backs of two straight chairs. She spread a folded quilt over the board and then smoothed a sheet over that. A row of black flatirons heated before the fire. She picked up one, with a thick pad of folded cloth wrapped around its handle so as not to burn her hand, and began to smooth out wrinkles in one of Guy's shirts. I liked the smell of the hot iron against the starched pieces.

I waited for her to touch a finger to her tongue and give it a quick pop to the bottom of the iron. If she didn't get a sizzle, she would give me the iron to press my doll clothes and reach for a hot one from the hearth. Now and then she rubbed her iron across a wrapper from Octagon soap. That cleared the starch that was sticking to it and made the iron move smoothly. While we ironed, I talked. She didn't seem to mind how much.

Occasionally Aunt Betty mumbled things like "Fanny needs to make her starch thinner" or "This iron's not hot enough."

There was only one bad thing about Aunt Betty living with us. She didn't seem to care for Ranger. She especially didn't like him in the house. I wondered if Ranger could sense her feeling. One night he refused to come in. Instead, he found a warm spot underneath the house by the kitchen chimney.

"That's better for him anyway," Mamma said. "The bricks stay hot long after the fire goes out. He's warmer there."

All the same, I missed lying beside him by the fire.

One day, while Aunt Betty and I were ironing, Clyde, Jr., came with his father. Uncle Clyde looked at Aunt Betty and me ironing and said, "Now, there's two of a kind."

I didn't like what he said. Aunt Betty was a rawboned, thin-as-a-slat person. She didn't look like anybody in our family. Besides, she drank coffee from her saucer and dipped snuff, which she kept in her apron pocket. What was worse, I didn't want to be an old maid.

Like it or not, Clyde, Jr., began calling me "Aunt Betty."

Every spring, Mamma did extra housecleaning. One of the major projects was sunning all the mattresses outdoors. Aunt Betty let it be known she did not want her bed disturbed, so Mamma didn't say anymore about it.

Not long afterward, one of Aunt Betty's relatives came to take her to a funeral. Mamma saw her chance, and we helped drag Aunt Betty's mattress outside.

"I don't want her to know about this," Mamma said, letting her look linger on me.

Days after, I yearned to tell Aunt Betty about the sunning. One day, as we ironed, I couldn't keep it in any longer.

"Mamma took your bed out in the yard while you were gone," I told her.

She let out a "Humph!"

I lowered my voice and described in every detail how we threw back the covers and dragged her mattress out and over two wooden sawhorses. Afterwards, I told her, we put it back just like she kept it with the pillows in a roll under her bedspread.

Though another "Umph" was all I got from her, I felt better. I would no longer pop from the secret.

If only that could have been the end of it! But I began to worry about being a tattletale. Finally, I confessed to Mamma.

"I figured she knew, the way she's been acting," Mamma replied. Then she looked me right in the eyes. "Dell," she said, "nobody likes a tattletale."

One day when I came home from school, Aunt Betty was gone. One of her relatives was sick and she was needed again. I missed her.

# ~27~
# Uncle John

Ranger's bark at the sound of a strange car woke us even before the horn blasted into the night air. I heard Mamma getting up, saw the flicker of the lamp come to life, and lay listening.

"Grace!" I recognized the voice. It was Uncle Clyde.

Mamma stood at the front door with the lamp when I heard him call out, "I didn't get out because of that dog."

"What's wrong?"

"John's dead. Some drunk shot him. We just got word."

Mamma's voice quivered like the cold air coming in the door. "I'll send Grady a telegram in the morning."

The car chugged back up the hill, and Mamma'a footsteps sounded in the kitchen.

Uncle John dead? Daddy's brother was Chief of Police in Hamlet, North Carolina. I thought about his wife, Aunt Josephine. And Grandma and Granddaddy. Did parents still love their children as much as Mamma loved us now?

The next morning at the train depot we watched the telegraph operator tap out the message in Morse code. Afterwards, we went to Grandma's.

Relatives and townspeople gathered in the parlor. Many brought dishes of food. With each arrival, someone retold "how it happened."

When Mamma said, "You children go on in the other room," all of us did except Woodrow, Great Aunt Rhiny's son who was a little older than Guy.

The house was otherwise quiet, so we could still hear the voices of the grown-ups in the next room.

"He went out in the country to answer a call about a man threatening to kill his family," a voice said. "He could have sent a deputy, but he knew the man and thought he could deal with him better."

"Sounds just like John," one of my aunts remarked.

A voice I didn't recognize said, "They say the fellow put a double-barreled shotgun through his car window and shot him before he ever got out."

Now and then Woodrow asked, "Who, Mamma?" Aunt Rhiny was so soft-spoken I could not hear her answer.

Then I heard Grandma. "I just hope the Lord takes me before I lose another one of my children." She sounded so sad. Tears welled in my eyes. She had answered my question. No matter their age, parents never stop loving their children.

Though friends continued to bring food, nobody seemed hungry. We children had not even gone to the pie safe for biscuits.

Daddy did not come home. He went straight from his work to Hamlet for the funeral. We didn't go since it was so far away.

That night as we sat around the fire thinking about the day, Mamma said suddenly, "I know one thing for sure. If I was Rhiny, I'd 'Who, Mamma' that Woodrow."

I knew what she meant. Adults believed children should be seen but not heard.

# ~28~
# Gaston

Most people in the 1930s did not take vacations. But Mamma took us many places other children did not get to visit. Besides our trips to Columbia, she often drove us to Charleston, over a hundred miles away. The museum was our favorite place. The shrunken heads of Pigmies gave me bad dreams, yet each time we visited I felt drawn to the glass case display. And, I couldn't wait to jump waves at the Isle of Palms on one of Mamma's spur-of-the-moment beach trips. I felt sorry for the children in my class who had seen the ocean only in pictures.

The trip we looked forward to most was to our Mack relatives in Gaston, a rural community south of Columbia—Mamma's birthplace. With only three stores, the town was even smaller than Ridge Spring. Still, it was exciting to be within walking distance of a store to get a bottle of Orange Crush from the big metal cooler filled with crushed ice. Some days we found enough empty bottles to trade for a drink.

Two of Mamma's sisters lived in Gaston. The oldest, Aunt Alice, did not have children, but she loved us as her own. Like Mamma, she told us stories.

Aunt Frances, Mamma's sister nearer her age, had six children of her own and a stepdaughter, Nevlyn. Nevlyn, who was oldest, preferred to draw or paint than to play. But, the others, four boys and two girls, were great fun.

My cousin Margie and I were born two weeks apart. At

an early age, Margie showed musical talent. I liked to sit on the long piano bench with her and listen to her play. Our biggest problem was the teasing of her two younger brothers, Robert and Joe Ben. Their goal in life, it seemed, was to make us miserable. They constantly pestered us, thumping our heads with their knuckles or trying to bend our fingers back. One day they took kittens to the upstairs porch, made parachutes from men's handkerchiefs, and dropped the frightened little animals down.

"Get lost!" Robert ordered when Margie and I tried to make them stop. "What we do is none of your beeswax."

"Anybody with any gum-ball brains could see they like it," Joe Ben added. "They're landing on their feet."

In spite of their toughness, the boys joined the rest of the Mack children in being afraid of lightning. At the first sound of thunder, they piled onto Aunt Frances' bed and rehearsed a long list of things forbidden to do during a lightning storm: playing with scissors or any metal object, standing by an open window or door, going barefoot outdoors, or being near trees.

"Lightning struck a house they lived in and caught it on fire," Mamma explained. "That's why they're afraid."

Aunt Frances had nurse's training, but like most women of the time she did not work after she married. Unlike Mamma, Aunt Frances was quiet and soft-spoken. She never scolded her children or even raised her voice. My cousins thought our loud, lively mother was fun.

Still in her twenties, Mamma liked to be in the middle of things. She loved swimming. Every afternoon we headed for a nearby pond.

Bryce, who was Guy's age, loved to tease Mamma, especially about her Crazy Water Crystals, a kind of medicine she took "for her health." She stirred the crystals in a glass of water until it fizzled and drank it.

"Aunt Grace is crazy!" Bryce yelled. "She drinks Crazy Water Crystals."

Though I never thought it was funny, Mamma threw her head back and laughed. "Awh, get out of here!" she scolded playfully.

To our amazement, the Macks had not only a six-seater outdoor privy, but a makeshift shower in a backyard shed. When rain filled the large drum on the shed roof, a day in the sun warmed the water enough to take the chill off.

They had a well in the yard like we did. But instead of a pulley mounted to a tall wooden frame with a bucket to haul the water up, they had a pump set low to the ground on a platform. Priming the pump was a skill the older children didn't want to share with us younger ones, but by watching we soon learned. We also learned that forgetting to leave water in the tin pitcher for the priming was unforgivable.

We were never at a loss for something to do. We played "Mother May I?" on the stairsteps and hide-and-go-seek in the house and outdoors, or we plucked scuppernongs from the thick bronze bunches and popped them into our mouths, enjoying the winy sweetness.

When we least expected it somebody yelled, "The Silver Meteor!" We lit out barefoot down the dusty road toward the railroad tracks. The new streamlined passenger diesel ran from Florida to New York, stopping only in big cities. Out of breath from the chase, we stood dumbfounded as the train streaked by like a bullet of silver.

In the evenings we had shadow shows. Aunt Frances let us tack up a sheet over the opened French doors. The older cousins started off the show by getting behind the sheet with a light and doctoring on a "patient." Usually Bryce would operate. The audience on the dark side rolled in laughter as the doctor brought up socks, forks, serving spoons, a screwdriver, rope, and anything else handy. All the while, the patient moaned and groaned.

Most of my memories of these early years were happy, but one got my feelings all tangled.

We were at the Baptist Church cemetery while our mothers cleaned the family plot. All of a sudden Robert yelled out, "Hey, ya'll look! Idella's dead! It says so right here on this gravestone."

The other children joined in. "Let's run from her!" somebody said. "She's a ghost!"

"That's not me!" I hollered at their backs as they darted around tombstones.

The adults didn't give much mind to the children's carrying on, but I went close to Mamma and whispered to her.

"Pshaw," she said. "They know better and you do too. Just act like it's the wind blowing." She went back to her weeding and talking to Aunt Frances.

I knew she meant for me to go on about my business and not pay their joking any attention, but I couldn't seem to make myself do that. Their words jabbed me like the pointed ends of jackstones. I sat down on a concrete curbing and pouted until Margie came to sit by me.

I might have been able to forget the incident had it not been for what hung above the mantelpiece in the room where we girls slept. In a large fancy frame was a death certificate in flowery handwriting like the old family Bible at Aunt Alice's. I knew it told about our grandmother's death, but I had never given it much thought. Now, as I tried to go to sleep, it kept drawing my eyes. Like the gravestone, it said "Idella Fallaw died July 8, 1912." I couldn't be that person—I wasn't even born! Why then, I wondered, did it give me such a creepy feeling?

# ~29~
# Miss Bessie

Even before Louise's first reader became mine, I loved words. I liked the way they could jingle and be happy, be quiet and sad, or loud and scary. I even liked the smell of paper they were printed on. Because of the way I felt about books, nothing could keep me from being excited when school started up again—not even having Miss Bessie for my second-grade teacher.

Like Miss Grace, Miss Bessie was an old maid. She had also taught Daddy. But Miss Bessie was not soft-spoken like Miss Grace, and she was strict..

"Don't expect to be coloring or quilting," Louise said.

"Yeah," Guy added, "your fun times are over."

Nothing they said dampened my eagerness as I returned those yellowing days of fall to the rows of scarred desks bolted to the floor.

At first, classmates were strangers again, most of us having been separated all summer. Girls clunked shyly to the chalkboard in new hightop shoes. Boys wriggled bare toes against the oily smell of the floor. But we soon found our voices. The jangle of the recess bell and the playground pulled us back into our old familiarity.

I learned that Miss Bessie did not feel good. In the early 1930s, doctors didn't really understand allergies. Miss Bessie's own treatment for her stuffed nose was to keep a pan of water on the pot-bellied stove so the air in the classroom would not be dry. She constantly wiped her nose with men's handkerchiefs—since there were no Kleenex in those days—and hung them behind the stove to dry out.

Even if Miss Bessie's reputation for class order had not kept us still, her appearance would have. She was a large woman and always wore dark colors. Her hair—jet black in spite of her age—was wound into a ball on the back of her neck. Her glaring looks made most of us quake. Only Blondell, who sat behind me as he had in first grade, dared defy her. He just couldn't sit still.

Miss Bessie's punishment was carried out with the long bamboo pole she kept on the floor behind her desk. Since she rarely got up, except to exchange her handkerchiefs, she would pick up the pole and move it in such a way as to make the tip of it hit the guilty person on the head. When Blondell *got it*, the swish past my ear and the whack that followed froze my blood. On occasion the cane tip did a rapid *thud-thump-thud*. I lived in fear Miss Bessie would miss Blondell and hit me.

Even adults seemed afraid of Miss Bessie—all, that is, except Mamma.

"If my children couldn't learn all twelve multiplication tables in second grade," she announced to whoever happened to be listening, "I'd go up to that school and give her a piece of my mind. But since they can, I'll just keep quiet."

We read aloud from *The Little Citizen*, our social studies

book, to learn about our state and country. We wrote paragraphs about what we could do for our country and felt proud.

"Line up for the spelling bee," Miss Bessie said each day just before school was out.

The bee was stressful for everyone, but poor spellers hated this time. If they ever managed by luck to work up to the head of the line, they landed right back at the end. Even good spellers got sent to the end for not following Miss Bessie's rules.

"Remember," she said before each bee, "pronounce the word. Break the word into syllables; spell each syllable as you say it; then spell the word all together. Last, pronounce the word again."

Down the line we went. "Auditorium. **Au**—A–U. **Di**—D–I. **To**—T–O. **Ri**—R–I. **Um**—U–M. Auditorium."

I never missed studying my spelling words. I also made sure I knew my multiplication tables although I had a hard time with the sevens and nines. I didn't want Mamma coming up to the school and raising cain about the work being too hard. I knew how she could fly off the handle.

One morning as she drove us to school she jerked the car to a stop on the winding dirt road. Leaning her head out of the car window, she shouted at the colored man who was plowing a cornfield. "How in the tarnation do you expect us to travel over this road with you plowing it up?"

The man pulled on the mule's traces with a "Whoa!" and took his hat off in respect. "Missus," he said in his soft drawl, "I got to turn this mule 'round somewhere befo' I can go down the next row."

"I don't give a hoot where you turn him around,"

Mamma flung back. "You'd better quit churning up these ruts. They're bad enough without a plow going over them."

No, I didn't want Mamma to get riled up with Miss Bessie. Even with the hard work and the fear of the bamboo pole, I still loved school.

At recess we played Pretty Girl Station. After we chose sides and drew our lines to stand on, each team decided what its occupation would be. Then both teams marched to the center. The other side would call out "Bum. Bum. Bum! Where are you from?"

We chanted, "Pretty Girl Station."

"What's your occupation?" they called back.

Without saying a word, we started acting out our occupation. We washed dishes, churned butter, shelled peas, picked cotton, or something everybody would be familiar with.

The others tried to guess what we were doing. If they got it right, we started running back to our line. Anybody who got caught had to join the opposing team. The side who had the most people when the bell rang for recess to end won the game.

I loved programs in the auditorium, upstairs in the big building. All eleven grades gathered for plays and singing. Mrs. Truluck led us in songs. I especially liked *rounds* like "Three Blind Mice" and "Row, Row, Row Your Boat."

One day as the first four grades marched back from the auditorium to our rooms for dismissal, I saw Mamma whip into the school yard to pick us up. To my surprise, she ran straight into the flagpole.

"Guy!" somebody hollered, "that's your mamma!"

The students started talking. The teachers looked at each

other in disbelief. I felt my face turn red.

Mamma put the car in reverse, backed up, and cut off the motor. Then she got out and looked the situation over. The fender was bent and the flagpole knocked crooked.

In my mind I could already hear Daddy's reaction. "Grace, how in the world," he would ask, "could you hit a flagpole on a school ground as big as that?"

I could imagine Mamma tossing her head back and laughing.

After that day, I never stood around the pole to pledge allegiance to the flag without remembering the day Mamma rammed it.

# ~30~
# Guy

"Dell," Mamma called, "run down to the barn and see what's keeping Guy. He should've been through milking long ago. It'll be dark soon."

I left my jigsaw puzzle of the thatched-roof cottage with the English garden and dashed out the door and down the wagon road.

Barn smells engulfed me as I headed toward Bittersweet's stall. The full milk pail sat outside the half door, but there was no sign of Guy. The scent of cigar was in the air. It made me think of Daddy.

I called out Guy's name, then stood still and listened. Above the barn sounds, I could hear moaning. I held my breath and followed the sound. Guy was on his knees, bent over in the hay, his face a sickly green.

Seeing me, he croaked, "Get Mamma—quick. I'm dying."

Moving faster than I thought I could run, I raced up the hill.

"Guy's dying!" I yelled at the top of my lungs. "Hurry! Guy's dying!"

Mamma was out the door and headed toward me before I reached the house, her apron strings flying behind her. I turned on my heel and led the way.

She had leaned over Guy and was feeling his head when she spied the problem and straightened up.

"Well, young man," she said, "it serves you right. I guess you had to learn the hard way."

She stooped over and picked up the stub of one of Daddy's cigars. "At least you know now what it tastes like."

With the milk pail in one hand, she helped Guy up with the other. "You won't die from it." Her voice didn't carry any sympathy. "But I expect it'll be a long time before you try to smoke again."

Guy didn't eat any supper. He lay on his bed with his head hung over the chamber pot until he finally fell asleep.

I worried about him. Mamma had been short tempered as she sometimes was with all of us when we fussed or did something she thought was foolish. "Don't you have common horse sense?" she'd ask. Still, I knew she loved us. She and Guy had a special kind of bond. Now that he was almost as tall as her five feet four inches, he would slip up behind her while she washed dishes and put his hands over her eyes.

"Guess who?" he asked, trying to disguise his voice.

"Nelson Eddy," she would say, using the name of one of her favorite singers.

"Nope."

"Gene Autry."

"Nope."

"Tom Sawyer."

"You're getting warm," he giggled.

On and on they'd go until the game wore thin and Guy asked, "Give up?"

Teasing Mamma was Guy's way of showing love. But I had not yet learned to give or accept teasing. Would I ever? I wondered.

One fall evening Mamma decided it was time to try out the blackberry wine she made to sprinkle over her fruit cakes. Louise begged for a taste but after a quick sip turned it down. I thought it looked too much like medicine. But Guy insisted on a small tumbler of his own. Holding his glass, he played the part of a drunk. He wobbled around the room and rattled on in a kind of gibberish as he recited, "The boy stood on the burning deck, eating peanuts by the peck."

Louise and I broke into gales of laughter until Mamma turned serious. "Let me tell you—if you had a father who drank, you wouldn't think being drunk was funny. Your daddy has his faults, but at least he's a teetotaller." She was right about that. Daddy didn't drink anything but water. He thought everything else tasted terrible. "If I need medicine," he said, "I'll take it."

Guy stopped acting drunk, but he was still in a good mood. He had been happier since he entered fourth grade and had Miss Harriet for his teacher.

This was Miss Harriet's first year teaching. She was young and pretty. Her hair, tucked up in golden curls, glowed like a halo when she was out on the playground. Her complexion was peaches and cream. Best of all, she smiled.

During recess, the boys in Miss Harriet's class played ball. The girls jumped rope, and she jumped with them. I liked to hear Guy tell about the stories they wrote in class. He wrote one pretending he was a grain of corn. He'd do anything for Miss Harriet.

Early in the school year Guy bit his tongue really bad playing football. Miss Harriet took a clean handkerchief and held it on the bitten place until it stopped bleeding. From then on, Guy loved her.

I didn't see how I could like school any more that I did already, but I couldn't wait to get to Miss Harriett's class.

# ~31~
# Bootlegger's House

When school let out one day in January, I didn't see Mamma anywhere. Guy, Louise, and I stood against the brick building trying to feel warmth stored from the weak sun. We watched children who lived on bus routes load noisy buses smelling of gasoline and those from town start walking home. Still, no sign of Mamma.

"Come on," Guy said. "Let's start walking." He pulled on his aviator cap, a black, oilcloth head cover with side flaps that snapped under his chin. He looked strange, as the tops of his ears bent over, making lumps under the flaps. Seeing him made me think of people from another planet like those in Flash Gordon serials. Even so, I envied Guy the warmth his cap offered. Louise and I never wore hats, and our long hair did little to protect our ears against the biting chill.

By the time we passed through town and started along the highway, I knew Mamma wasn't coming. We had no choice but to continue the mile-and-a-half trek home.

Nobody carried bookbags at our school. Guy's and Louise's books kept slipping from their arms. I held my reader and tablet across my chest, pressing my coat against me. That helped shield my body from the cold wind.

Farther down the paved road we neared a house I dreaded passing. I wanted to walk on the other side of the highway, but Guy said we had to face traffic so we would know when to get out of the way of the occasional car.

Shrubbery covered the front of the house except for a dark hole at the door. I had heard whispers of "She's not right" about the woman who lived there with her parents. They said she still acted like a child. Passing the house was scary for me. How did she look? How did she act? Somehow I knew I would never ask or get the answers to my questions.

Just beyond the house Guy said the words I feared. "Come on. We're taking the shortcut." He turned onto the clay road on our left.

My heart beat fast. Cold air stung my face. We would pass the bootlegger's house. I wasn't sure just exactly what a bootlegger did or how he did it. But I did know he kept his homemade *still*, where he made his moonshine, hidden from the law.

Once we got far enough down the road, we could see our house sitting way over in the valley. In a field between it and the road was the bootlegger's house with all of its dark, scary secrets.

Louise and Guy walked faster than I did. I tried my best

to keep up. I didn't want to be lagging behind when we reached that house. We didn't take lunch to school and none was served, so I was hungry as well as cold and tired. By the time we cut across the field, my legs felt as stiff as the leftover cornstalks crunching beneath our shoes.

"Don't go close to the house!" I called out. But they didn't seem to hear me.

My stomach twisted in a tight knot as we drew nearer. I held my breath and looked out across the barren farmland. And then my head seemed to turn all by itself toward the bootlegger's.

Glass jars—more than I had ever seen, even with all Mamma's canning—were lined up against the back of the house. Suddenly, flashes of light bounced off the jars. For a moment I was blinded. My chest ached. Then I realized I was still holding my breath.

Did the bootlegger have the power to stun trespassers with rays like in the picture show? As tired as I was, I took off running until I caught up. I knew my stockings were picking up beggar's-lice from the prickly weeds along the furrows, but I didn't care.

Ranger saw us coming and ran to meet us. He leaped and wriggled around Guy and Louise and then lapped my face and hands with his warm tongue. I was safe.

"That dad-blamed car wouldn't start," Mamma said. "I think the battery's dead, but Pete's off in the wagon, and I didn't have anybody to help me push it."

We sat at the table eating fried chicken, rice and gravy, and butter beans when Louise said, "It wouldn't be so bad to have to walk home if Idella wasn't such a scaredy cat."

"Yeah," Guy added, "she thinks the bootlegger catches

little girls and puts them in his moonshine."

"Guy—" Mamma scolded.

The sight of the bootlegger's jars stuck in my mind like the beggar's-lice on my stockings until Pete came back. Then we all got behind the car and pushed while Mamma steered and worked the throttle. The motor fired up, and she left it running until we got ready to go to church where Miss Katie's stories made my world a wonderful place.

# ~32~
# Summer Days

Clyde, Jr., and I liked to make penny shows. First, we dug a shallow hole and lined it with blooms from petunias, the four o'clock bush, and yellow bells. Then we placed a piece of glass over the flowers. Carefully we mounded dirt over the edges and sprinkled a smattering of sand over the glass, hiding a view of the flowers.

"Go find people to come see our show," Clyde, Jr., said.

"What if they don't have a penny?"

"Tell them to find a pretty piece of broken glass or a smooth rock."

Once I convinced Guy, Louise, and our mothers to come, Clyde, Jr., and I took turns smoothing away the dirt so the audience—one by one—could view our pretty collection of blooms.

If we didn't go to Old Shoals on the sweltering days, Mamma set out washtubs of water to warm in the sun for us to play in. Afterwards, we bathed Ranger. His toenails scraped the ribbed tin sides and a whine lay at the back of his throat. He couldn't wait to get out and shake.

Now and then I slipped into the smokehouse for privacy to make believe. The smell of ashes from the curing fire mixed with that of the remaining sausage links hanging over the rafters. Sometimes I took my dolls and told them stories.

Our cousins liked to come to the farm in summer, and Mamma let them. Lithco was a regular visitor. When his family came on Sundays, he begged to stay even though he didn't have a change of clothes.

"Oh, we'll find him some," Mamma said.

Sometimes his sister Peggy, who was younger than I, stayed too. She liked Guy best of all. He tickled her and she giggled.

"That's enough of that giggling!" Mamma called out from the kitchen, but it kept up.

A highlight of the summer was the visit from our Gaston kin, in spite of the boys' jumping out from behind doors to scare us or catching the sun with a mirror and shining it in our eyes.

With every bang of the screen door, Mamma called, "Stay in or out!"

Even though we'd been told of "dog days," the mid-summer season when scrapes and cuts have a hard time healing, we scooted all over the place barefoot, even around the barn. In the pasture we gave Tarzan yells beneath tangles of wild grape vines and waded in the stream to cool off.

Back in the yard, Bryce and Guy made guns from a piece of sawed plank, a clothespin, and a strip of rubber cut from an old inner tube. We talked on telephones made of wire and tin cans. Like the tall man on stilts at the fair, we punched holes in larger tin cans, ran strings through to hold on to, and walked on them.

Catching June bugs was my least favorite pastime. Some of the cousins carried their pet June bugs around in a matchbox. When the bugs were let out to fly, a piece of sewing thread tied to a back leg kept them from getting away.

"Idella's a baby!" the boys taunted when I said I didn't want a June bug.

To avoid their taunts I held on to a string, flinching each time the bug lit on my shoulder and fastened its strong spiny legs into my clothing. If I let him go and he got away, he would carry the string all his life. I didn't want that to happen so I suffered through it.

I liked it when we put on shows. Louise was the popular choice to go first with her one-man show. She made ugly faces by crossing her eyes and hooking her thumbs in the sides of her mouth. Using her index fingers, she dragged down the outside corners of her eyes. She made us all laugh.

"All right, young lady," Mamma said when she caught a glimpse of her, "you're going to freeze that way one day and then you'll be in a pickle."

"That Louise is a card," Aunt Frances added.

On my turn I put on one of Mamma's dresses and her high heels and told stories.

One afternoon we all piled in the car and drove to a field to see a lady parachute from an airplane. Ever since 1927, when Charles Lindbergh made the first solo, nonstop flight across the Atlantic Ocean, everybody was fascinated with airplanes.

In a daring act, the lady jumped from the small plane, pulled the rip cord on her parachute, and glided down into the open field. Afterwards she pulled off her aviator cap and shook out her curly blonde hair. Holding out her cap, she moved around the crowd to receive donations.

"One of these days," Louise announced on the way home, "I'm going to jump out of a plane just like that."

On most days that the Macks were there, Mamma took us to Old Shoals where the boys slid dangerously on the rocks.

Back at home, at dark, somebody would yell, "Time for ghost stories!" And we'd build a backyard fire to use for light. The flames from the fire played hide-and-seek with the darkness at the edge of the yard, creating shadows that moved among us like living things.

Usually Bryce would start the storytelling. From the moment he moaned, "I want my toe," shivers ran up my spine. Tension mounted. Would Bryce pick me to jump at with "I've GOT my toe!"?

Later, we all slept on pallets in Guy's bedroom. The boys always started kidding each other and making noise.

"All right," Aunt Frances cautioned in her mild-mannered way. "Stop that cutting the fool and go to sleep."

But I couldn't go to sleep. I lay wide awake watching the shadows on the ceiling and listening for ghosts from the stories to creak the floorboards. In spite of the fear the tellings around the campfire brought, I looked forward to the following night and a new mixture of pleasure *and pain*.

*Guy, Louise, and Idella with Daddy. Apple tree in far left corner. Taken the year electricity came to our farm.*

*Idella, Louise, and Guy in back yard of country home. Louise "rode" her horse in the crook of the tree at the corner of the house. In left background is the well and the tree with roots used for my playhouse. Fanny's washtubs were set up by this tree.*

Guy — 6th grade.

Louise — 5th grade.

Idella — 4th grade.

*Taken at our 4th-grade class Easter party. Blondell, who "milked the cow" with my curls in 3rd grade, sits in lower left corner. Miss Harriett is in upper right corner. That's me on the 2nd row from the top, near the right side of the window.*

*Guy (in knickers) with classmates at recess.*

*My cousin Clyde, Jr., from Ridge Spring.*

*My cousin Margie from Gaston.*

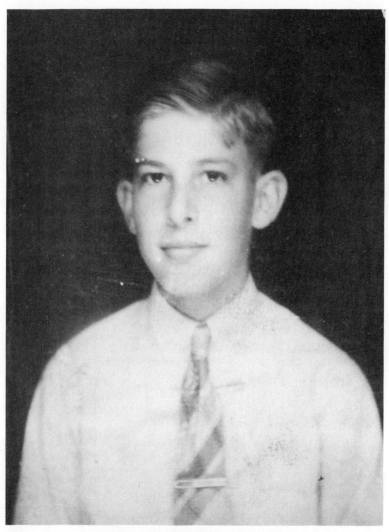

*Jimmy at 13, when we met at peach shed.*

*Daddy and Mamma, 1937.*

# ~33~
# Chickens

Mamma was proud of her chickens, especially the laying hens like Rhode Island Reds and White Plymouth Rocks. Like other farm wives, she told visitors how many setting hens—those sitting on eggs to hatch biddies—she had and how many eggs she gathered daily.

I liked to watch Mamma feed the chickens. When she threw dried corn to them, they rushed toward it, wings flapping, swooping in one direction and then another in unison like they were fastened together.

If a hen didn't lay many eggs, that one was the first to be baked for Sunday dinner. Then there were the younger chickens, called broilers, grown for frying.

When the killing time came, I tried to avoid seeing it. Like the butchering, it bothered me. Most farms had a block behind the woodpile for cutting off chickens heads. Once the choice was made and the chicken was caught, his head was laid on the block. Strangely, his body seemed to go into a trancelike state as he waited for the sharp hatchet to come down. Floride never used the block. Instead, she rang the broilers' necks. I couldn't bear to watch.

Afterwards, scalding water loosened feathers for plucking. A lighted newspaper singed off any small feathers that remained. If the chicken was to be fried, it was cut into pieces, including the pulley bone for making wishes. "It's my turn to pull for a wish," usually started a fuss at the table.

I was afraid of the roosters. They strutted around with high steps as if they owned the place. I was especially afraid of Guy's bantam rooster. In spite of its small size, I had seen the bantam rooster rise up on tiptoes, spread his wings, stretch his neck, and leap into the air.

Once I had to jump up the steps to the asparagus packing house to get away from him. The spurs on his legs were sharp, and I knew he would chase me if I stepped down. So, I just stood in the doorway and called to Guy as he sat hammering on something. "Come get your rooster."

The little rooster kept craning his head forward, tilting it to one side and then the other, and peering at me as if he was making plans about what to do to me.

Guy kept hammering away. Finally, I yelled out to Mamma in the house. "Make Guy get his rooster!"

For the first time Guy looked my way. "All you've got to do is ease down and walk by him like you're not afraid," he said."If you run, he's going to chase you."

I knew he was right, but I couldn't make myself do it. I called Mamma again. With a disgusted look, Guy threw down his hammer, walked over to his rooster, and picked him up. Running his hand over the colorful little tail feathers that ended in a furl, Guy put him on the ground and the little rooster strutted off in another direction.

# ~34~
# Mamma's Ship

Summer was slipping away.

A slow rain made our front porch a special place. I turned one of the big rockers around, leaned it against the wall, and draped a quilt over it. Beneath it I sat daydreaming.

The light pattering of raindrops and the smell of fresh earth had almost put me to sleep when Mamma, Guy, and Louise came out onto the porch. Ranger followed and lay down with his back against the house.

"Look!" Louise said. "The devil is beating his wife with a frying pan."

I knew she meant the sun was shining through the rain. I peeked out from my cocoon. The golden drizzle enclosed the porch in a comforting circle.

Mamma started half humming, half singing "When Johnny Comes Marching Home," one of her World War I songs. Though Daddy had been too young to fight in the war, Mamma knew all the songs.

"When my ship comes in," she said, with a faraway look in her eye, "I'm going to buy us a piano."

I understood Mamma was talking about having money, for she had read us the story of Dick Whittington, an orphaned servant boy in London. A merchant who sent ships out with goods to be sold allowed each of his servants to send a possession for sale. Since Dick had only a cat, he reluctantly sent it. After a long voyage, the ship arrived in a land over-run with rats.

"I will give half my kingdom to anyone who can rid my castle of rats," the king announced.

The captain of the ship immediately sent for Dick's cat. The king was so happy when the cat chased the rats away, he sent Dick Whittington one of the largest fortunes ever known to man.

When I finished dreaming about that, Mamma was singing another War song: "When she wore a tulip, a bright yellow tulip, and I wore a big red rose."

"Do the one about Paris," Guy begged.

Mamma laughed and belted out, "How you gonna keep her down on the farm after she's seen Paree?"

I thought about the times Mamma woke us up with a World War I bugle song: "You gotta get up! You gotta get up this morning!" Like the soldiers, Louise would come back with "Someday I'm going to murder the bugler; someday you're going to find him dead."

We left the War songs behind and started singing hymns. Mamma gave us the pitch in her soprano voice and switched to alto on "Dwelling in Beulah Land." We sang "What a Friend We Have in Jesus" and "Bringing in the Sheaves."

At some point during the concert the devil stopped beating his wife with the frying pan. The sun turned the sky pink, then purple, and from purple to gray.

After we sang "Billy Boy," a ballad about a wife who was too young to leave her mother, Louise said, "Let's sing the gypsy songs."

We started with "Shanty Town" and moved on to "Birmingham Jail," about a man who said, "If I had wings of an angel, over these prison bars I would fly and into the arms of my sweetheart. Then I'd be ready to die."

That one was sad, but the saddest was yet to come. It was a song about a little girl named Mary Fagin who lived in England when children worked in factories. Although she got only pennies for her week's work in the pencil factory, someone killed her and took her money.

Shadows climbed, ribboning the porch in half-light. Our voices became part of the dusky evening. We sang on in the warm southern darkness, tree frogs chorusing in the lulls. A half-moon rose over the cornfield and silvered our yard. Stars twinkled in the velvet sky.

On the way inside to get ready for bed, Mamma sang, "Pack up your troubles in your old kit bag and smile, smile, smile"—another of her World War I favorites.

We spent lots of evenings singing together on the porch. I couldn't imagine life without Mamma.

# ~35~
# Third Grade

The year I entered third grade, I began reading the Bobbsey Twins books. I went with the twins to the mountains and the seashore. When I finished one book and waited impatiently for another, I imagined the characters having all kinds of adventures without me. I still liked for Mamma to read to me, but my dream of reading myself had come true. I couldn't get enough of it.

In the southern custom, we called all our women teachers "Miss" even if they were married. This year, we had Miss Etta. Like Miss Bessie, Miss Etta was strict. She was also strong on manners. If any child entered third grade without responding to elders with "Yes, Ma'am" and "No, Ma'am," Miss Etta made sure that lesson was learned before the year ended.

Miss Etta believed in cleanliness. "You may not be able to learn all your lessons," she said, "but all of you have soap and water." Constantly she cautioned us to keep our hands away from our faces.

I found the germs Miss Etta talked about as mysterious as her hind vision. "You had better be quiet when I turn to write on the blackboard," she said, "because I have eyes in the back of my head."

Finally, I figured it out. Miss Etta divided her reddish-brown hair down the middle and plaited it on the sides of her head. Then she wound each plait into a coil at the nape of her neck. The hind eyes *had* to be in those circles of hair.

On entering her classroom in the morning, we were expected to go directly to the cloakroom and hang up our coats. Children who brought lunches put the brown paper bags, many dotted with grease spots from peanut butter, on the shelf above their coats. Once, a boy had to be ordered to remove his coat.

Again this year Blondell sat behind me. Our desks were joined, front to back, together in rows. Though Miss Etta never saw him and I dared not tell, he played "milk the cow" with my sausage-like curls that fell just above his desk. At least, I told myself, when Blondell got into trouble now, the threat of the bamboo cane was gone.

One day when Miss Etta stepped outside the door to speak to another teacher, Blondell grabbed my pencil and held it away from me. What if Miss Etta came back in and I did not have my pencil? I panicked and jumped up to reach for it. Blondell scooted out the other side of his desk, clutching my pencil over his head. Without thinking, I ran to the end of the row and around to where he stood. At the moment I reached him, Miss Etta walked through the door. With her eyes glued on me, Blondell climbed quickly into his seat.

The room was suddenly so quiet you could hear a pin drop. Everybody was looking at me. Miss Etta stood like a statue.

"Idella," she asked, "would you have gotten out of your seat if I had been in the room?"

"No, Ma'am," I managed to reply. My heart was broken. I had been called down by a teacher!

I slipped quietly back into place.

Blondell still had my pencil. What if he licked the lead the way I'd seen him do his? My stomach churned until Miss Etta turned to write on the board and Blondell dropped my pencil over my shoulder and into my lap. I vowed never, ever to forgive him.

Even with Blondell pestering me, I loved being in school. I liked the way light came through the high bare windows of our room, moved over the ceiling, and fell across the racks of maps. Most of all, I loved our reading book with its wonderful stories and poetry.

The beautiful rhythm of poems like "Hiawatha" touched me. I read and reread "The Lamplighter" in which Robert Louis Stevenson tells how he watched from his window in Scotland as the man lit the gas streetlamps. Since Stevenson was sick much of the time and had to stay in bed, he wrote, "When I am stronger, I'll go round at night and light the lamps with you."

We memorized lots of poems. I still remember some of them. There was one I liked with the lines, "There's nothing so kingly as kindness, and nothing so royal as truth." I looked forward to standing before the class and reciting our memory work. I was not my shy self then but an actress on a stage.

That same year something happened that made me worry about speaking before an audience again. For the Christmas program at school, Miss Etta gave me three pages to memorize. I would recite it in the auditorium in front of the whole school.

I was not nervous as I stood on the stage by myself, the red velvet curtain drawn behind me. I had practiced so much I could recite my speech in my sleep, but somewhere in my story, something went terribly wrong. All of a sudden, everybody laughed. My speech was not meant to be funny. Why were they laughing? As I looked out, I recognized a senior who went to our church. He laughed so hard he almost fell from his seat. My mind went blank. From behind the curtain Miss Etta gave me the next word. *I had had to be prompted!* I was horrified.

Later, I learned that I had said "Jesus made the blind people hear, and the deaf people see."

That wasn't the only thing that happened while I was in Miss Etta's class that left a bad memory. I was still getting over the events of Halloween.

I had never heard of "Trick or Treat." As far as I knew, none of the other children had either. Yet there was something about Halloween night, with the fluffy clouds floating across the moon, that conjured up images of witches riding on broomsticks.

Mamma drove us to Grandma's and allowed us to play along the railroad track with other neighborhood children. The tarry smell of the crossties was strong as we headed up the track toward town. Rails reflected the cold silvery light of the moon.

Suddenly somebody yelled, "Hey, there's Miss Etta's house! Let's bomb it!"

"Yeah!" somebody else called out. "She's mean. She makes us take off and put on our coats every time we go in and out of the building."

One of the boys scooped up handfuls of gravel from the railroad. Others followed—including me.

Like ghosts in the night, we flew along the oak-lined street, dodging in and out of hedges near her porch.

*PING. ZING. CLUNK.* We peppered her house with gravel.

The outside lights came on. We darted like crazy behind shrubs and bushes. Frozen like in a game of tag freeze, we peeked through. The door opened. Miss Etta stepped out. She looked around, then turned and went back inside.

I had a hard time going to sleep that night. I didn't hate Miss Etta. Why had I done that?

If Miss Etta knew who was in the bushes that Halloween night, she never let on. For the rest of the school year I felt guilty. I wanted to tell her I was sorry, but I didn't know how to bring it up.

# ~36~
# Mamma's Permanent

Mamma was particular about how she looked. She never went to bed without putting Pond's Cold Cream on her face.

"Please don't put that stuff on your face until I kiss you goodnight," I'd beg. Mamma thought that was funny, but she hadn't tried to kiss a cheek that was slick and smelly.

Now that she was thirty years old, Mamma decided she wanted a new look. She had her hair cut when Guy was a baby and had worn it in a short, straight "bob" ever since. Today, she planned to get a permanent wave. At the Batesburg beauty parlor it cost two dollars.

As usual, Louise, Guy, and I went to the picture show. When the movie was over, we walked next door and up the stairs to the beauty parlor—the way we always did when Mamma was getting her "bob" shampooed and trimmed. She was always through before the movie ended, but she stayed and talked with the ladies there until we got out.

Climbing the stairs we suddenly smelled rotten eggs. Guy turned on his heel and ran back down the steps. Louise grabbed her nose, but she and I walked on in. A lady was under the dryer, but I didn't see Mamma. Then I heard the familiar voice. "Here!" she said. "It's burning over here."

I couldn't believe my eyes. Mamma was in the corner of the room hooked up to a bulky electric machine with cords coming down from somewhere up above. The beautician stood beside her, fanning her head with a folded newspaper.

Mamma's face was fiery red. Then I saw that her hair had been wrapped around little metal rods hooked to clamps on the ends of the electric cords.

"I'm going back in the picture show," Louise said. Her voice sounded funny because she was still holding her nose. "Y'all come get me when you're ready."

I knew the manager would let the three of us back in the show. We had already paid our dimes; they didn't care how many times we sat through it. But I wasn't going to leave Mamma. What if all her hair burned off? What if she were electrocuted and died?

As I watched, Mamma pointed to another spot on her head and the beautician fanned there. "It won't be long now," the woman comforted.

After what seemed forever, the electric current was turned off and the curlers allowed to cool. Then, one by one, the clamps were unlocked, leaving them dangling from the cords, which looked like slithering snakes.

When the curlers were removed from Mamma's head, it was covered with a tangle of tight curls. She didn't look like herself. The beautician rinsed her hair with water and combed it. It was so frizzy!

"That's all you have to do to it," the lady instructed. "Just wet your comb in a glass of water and comb."

I didn't like it. I knew Daddy wouldn't either. But at least Mamma was all right except for her blistered face.

As Mamma and I waited at the door of the picture show for Guy and Louise, I felt my face flush. I just knew everybody was looking at her.

Guy came out of the show first. When he saw Mamma, he gave a funny grin. Louise grabbed her nose again.

The stench of the permanent solution seemed even stronger as we closed ourselves up in the car for the ride home.

"Mamma," Louise asked as we started off, "can't I roll down this window?"

"No, my hair's still damp," Mamma told her. "I don't want a draft on my head."

We had no choice but to endure the breathtaking smell for the entire nine long miles.

# ~37~
# Milking

*Ching-choo. Ching-choo.* Guy leaned forward as he sat on the milking stool, the side of his face pressed against old Bittersweet's brown-speckled hide. He squeezed and pulled at two of the cow's teats, first with one hand and then the other. The tugging had to be hurting the swollen udder with its bulging veins. I didn't like to look.

Milk covered the bottom of the tin pail, and the steady rhythm changed to *shig, shig.* It grew deeper and deeper as the pail filled. Foam rose from the twin streams.

The smell of warm milk mingled with barn odors. My stomach sloshed like the milk in the bucket.

Bittersweet pulled fodder from the rack in her lazy way and swished her tail close to my head.

"Shoo that fly before Bittersweet kicks the bucket over," Guy ordered. "And move back."

Since Guy was four years older, he didn't like me following him around. That's why I was surprised when he said,

"Come over here. I'm going to teach you how to milk."

I drew back, but he grabbed my arm and sat me down on the milking stool.

"Reach under there and get hold of her teats."

My stomach lurched. I couldn't do it.

"Go ahead." He settled on his haunches beside me, caught hold of my hands, and shoved them around Bittersweet's rubbery skin.

I cringed, but Guy kept saying, "Pull! Squeeze!" Somehow I managed to pull and squeeze, again and again. No milk.

Finally, he reached down and grabbed up the milk pail. "Awh, let's go," he said. "You'll never learn to milk."

He slipped the rope from Bittersweet's neck and with his foot pushed open the stall door to let her into the pasture.

At the sight of us, hogs in the nearby pen gathered around their trough, rooting and grunting. They were always hungry.

We trekked up the wagon road the short distance to the house.

Guy set the milk bucket on the table. "I tried to teach Idella how to milk," he announced, "but she never will learn."

I didn't want to think about what I had done. I didn't even want to think about where milk came from. I went to my room to play with my gray schoolteacher ledger.

Even though I didn't want to learn to milk, I did wonder why Bittersweet's milk hadn't come for me. Did she not like me? Then one day I learned the truth.

Guy was under the shed talking to Pete and laughing. I heard him say, "Idella didn't even know I had already milked her dry."

I started to run tell on him. But then I remembered how

Mamma felt about tattletales. It was the same way Aunt Josephine felt about a lazy bone. To use Aunt Josephine's word, Mamma *abhorred* tattletales. I would later grow to abhor them too.

# ~38~
# The Land

In spring I sat on a furrow between cotton fields watching field hands chop cotton. They worked their way up and down rows, thinning out cotton plants. Their hoes struck the ground with downward chops. A backward stroke took away one small plant; a forward, another. Now and then a hoe struck a rock, making a clanking sound.

*Chock! Chock! Clunk!* The chopping kept time with their song:

> *Ev'rybody livin' got to die, got to die,*
> *De rich and de poor, de short and de tall,*
> *All got to meet at de judgment hall.*
> *Ev'rybody livin' got to die, got to die.*

One voice called out in song and others joined in. Colorful bandannas on the women's head picked up the sunlight.

I ached to chop cotton, but Daddy stood firm. Louise and I were not allowed in the fields.

Little waves of heat shimmered up around me as I squinted my eyes against the sun. Then an idea popped into my head.

Back in our yard, I got a hoe from the shed and took it up by the apple tree. I would start my own garden. I chopped the ground the way I had seen the field hands do, getting rid of the weeds. Finally my plot of ground was nice and soft. I loved the smell of the fresh dirt. I went to find Mamma to ask her what I could plant.

Floride was changing bed sheets. Louise kept teasing her by falling onto the bed so she couldn't get the sheets off. Finally, Floride rolled her up in a sheet and plopped her in a rocker. Both of them were giggling.

"Louise," Mamma called from the front porch where she knocked down cobwebs with the broom, "stop aggravating Floride and go on outside and play."

I told Mamma about my garden. "You can dig up some dusty millers out by the four o'clock bush," she said. "They're too thick anyway."

I went to work digging up and planting the dusty-looking plants in my soft dirt. They made me think of the miller all covered with flour. I could still hear the field hands singing and laughing and talking. As I worked, I pretended I was one of them.

Soon Mamma came out with some zennia and marigold seeds she had dried from last year and told me how deep to plant them. I knew I wouldn't like the smell of the marigolds, but they would have pretty yellow flowers.

At the well I let the bucket down just enough to fill it halfway. A full one would be too heavy for me to pull up by the chain. With both hands I drew the chain through the pulley until I could swing the bucket over to sit on top of the well boards. Taking the dipper from its nail hook, I scooped up a cool drink. The water tasted just like the tin dipper.

After I had watered my garden, I remembered the small cedar trees beyond the walnut tree at the front of our house. Maybe I could dig up one and plant it in the corner of my garden.

Floride was shaking out a rug over the porch banisters when she saw me looking at the cedar trees.

"Honey, child," she called, "you don't want a cedar tree in your garden. You plant one and let it grow big enough to shade your grave, you gone die."

I never planted any cedar trees, but from then on every year that we lived in the country I had my own garden.

## ~39~
# Lossie

Pete didn't talk much. He just went about his work, but I knew he liked us. He let us watch him grease the axles on the wagon wheels and back up the mules to hitch them up. Sometimes he let us sit with him on the high wagon seat and ride into the fields.

Once I was near his house when he was cooking fatback. He came out on the porch with the strong smell of bacon following him.

"Little Missy," he called, "you want some fatback?"

He held up a plate of white meat fried to a crisp. I sat on the edge of his porch and dangled my legs while we ate the salty strips and sucked on the skin.

"It sho is fine to have meat hanging in the smokehouse," he said, fingering his tasty piece.

For the first time I noticed his fingernails had ridges like the seams Mamma's sewing machine made.

"Yes, siree, bob tail," he repeated, "it sho is fine."

I had always imagined Pete lived alone in his two-room house. I had never thought about him having any family but ours. That was why it was such a surprise the day his two daughters appeared. Nobody told me where Lossie and Flossie had been living or why they had come to stay with their father. But, I couldn't have been happier.

Lossie, the younger one, was nearer my age. She was plump, while Flossie was tall and thin. Lossie liked to talk; Flossie mostly nodded or shook her head, which was covered over with tight little braids.

"You want to play house?" I asked Lossie the first time I saw her. She grinned and followed me to the back porch where I had set up a cardboard box and made different rooms of a house in it. From last year's Sears, Roebuck catalog I had cut out members of a family.

We sat on the floor by the water bucket table, which held our dipper and wash pan, and played for hours.

"This is the mamma," I told her, holding up a pretty blond-haired lady. "And this is the daddy." Dressed in a suit and tie, the daddy carried something like a small suitcase. In order of their ages, I introduced Lossie to the brother, sister, and baby girl.

Lossie didn't seem to mind that all the people in the family were white, but for the first time I wondered why there were no pictures of colored families in the catalog. One day after Lossie had gone home, I asked Mamma about it.

"That's just the way it is," she said without turning from the flour she was sifting.

In the days that followed, Lossie and I gave our catalog family things we did not have: a radio, a washing machine with rollers to squeeze water out of clothes, and a stove that cooked with kerosene. We cut out electric fans to cool the rooms and put rugs on the floors. We gave the girl a carriage for her doll and the boy a bicycle.

I would tell Lossie which people to speak for and what to say. She repeated it. Time flew.

The only thing that bothered me at our play was the long strip of fly paper hanging just inside the screened door. When the flies' feet caught in the sticky substance, an awful buzzing kept up until the wings got caught too. I hated hearing it.

Sometimes we left our make-believe family to go outdoors. We picked sourgrass, stripped its leaves, and sucked tart juiciness from the stems. Other times we took my dolls to the cornfield and made them hair from the corn tassels—sometimes silky white; other times, black.

Mamma brought out milk and cookies for snacks and almost always sent food home by Lossie. Lossie never stayed to eat with me, though I wanted her to. I wished she could go to my school and my church. I could not understand why she didn't.

"That's just the way things are" was the only explanation I ever got.

I worried about Lossie and Flossie. Nobody had much in those days, but they had less than all the people I knew. Mamma saw to it they had clothes, but at Christmas Santa Claus left them only a bag of candy in a dresser drawer.

I did not understand the way things were, but I was clear on one thing: Lossie was my dear friend. I loved her.

## ~40~
# Porky

Daddy came home. As soon as he arrived, he was needed at the barn. Bittersweet had a calf due, and a sow a litter of pigs. One morning before school Daddy called us to the barn to see the long-legged wobbly calf. We stroked its velvet hide and listened to its thin bawl.

We knew the birth of pigs would be a different matter. We would never be allowed to handle piglets. That's why I was surprised on a Saturday morning to hear a pig's squeal at the back door.

In moments we crowded around Daddy and the ball of white smudged with pink that he carried in his arms. The piglet's forked feet flailed in the air with each high-pitched cry.

"The brood sow rolled over on this one," Daddy said. "Doubt he'll make it."

That was all Mamma needed to hear. She reached out for the squealing pig, curled him up in her apron, and held him close. He gave several little grunts and quieted down.

"He'd never be able to fight his way to the chow line with his bad leg," Daddy added. "She had eight."

"Get that cardboard box in the pantry, Weezie," Mamma said. She bundled the pig up in an old towel and put him in the box near the stove. Taking off her apron, she said, "I'm going to run into town and get a nipple."

Like Mamma, Ranger was always glad to ride to town.

Guy and I rode with Mamma while Louise watched after our pig.

From a nipple placed on a coca cola bottle, "Porky" drank Bittersweet's milk and grew. Soon we started taking him outside to let him root in the dirt.

The only problem was his back leg. He limped. Louise decided she would take care of that. She picked out some thin slats from the woodpile, tore strips of cloth from a flour sack, and made a splint for his leg.

I don't know whether Porky started putting his leg down because the splint was too heavy to hold up, or if it felt better. But after a while he walked with only a slight limp, and Louise took off the splint.

Soon Porky was following us around the yard. Like Ranger had learned to do, he ignored the chickens pecking all about. And, he never went back to the barnyard.

Louise's success with Porky's leg must have given her confidence in her skills as a doctor. When my doll's crying box broke, she talked me into letting her operate. I watched her cut open my doll's cloth body and work on the little metal circle in her back. Unfortunately, she couldn't fix it. Nothing could be done but to get sewing thread and sew her back up. My doll never cried again.

## ~41~
## The Fourth of July

Guy was born on the Fourth of July. When Mamma started having family reunions on the Fourth, Louise and I complained.

"That's not fair," Louise said.

"We don't have parties on our birthdays," I added.

Actually, we knew better than to fuss about it. The truth was Mamma loved being around people, and the Fourth was a good time to celebrate.

With plans underway, Pete and Daddy pulled the long asparagus tables out under the oaks. Fanny *blue*d out sheets for tableclothes.

The evening before the Fourth, Daddy, Uncle Clyde, and Uncle Dan barbecued a pig. Most of the night they tended the roasting over a hickory fire. When Mamma sent Louise and me to bed, we watched from our window. Now and then a shadow passed between us and the fire as one of the men got up to baste the pig with pungent sauce. We could hear the mumble of talking and laughing.

With the first crack of daylight, we were up and asking "When are they coming, Mamma?" and "How long now?"

"Any time," she kept repeating, and we strained our ears to listen for the sound of a car. Unlike Christmas with just Daddy's family, all of Mamma's relatives would come too. I couldn't wait.

When the cars did start pouring in, Mamma rushed from

the kitchen to greet each load with a loud whoop. Daddy had harrowed the sunflowers from the field beyond the apple tree, and cars pulled in haphazardly to park on the hill.

With each new arrival, there was kissing and hollering and laughing. We children were squeezed and told, "I never would have known you."

The Macks and Aunt Alice and Uncle Elliott always came from Gaston. Aunt Alice would climb from their car with her arms open. I loved her hugs even if I did nearly suffocate from her talcum powder and perfume. Another of Mamma's sisters, Aunt Adele, and her family came from Cayce. Mamma's brother, Uncle Rob, and his wife, Aunt Bernelle, drove down from Columbia. Many from Daddy's family—most of them from close-by—were there too.

Talking and laughing in loud, happy voices, the women carried baskets of food to the tables. Platters of fried chicken and baked ham, bowls of potato salad, pimento cheese sandwiches, deviled eggs, macaroni and cheese, sliced tomatoes, homemade pickles, and every kind of dessert: sweet potato pie, luscious chocolate and lemon meringue pies, chocolate layer cake, Japanese fruitcake, Lady Baltimore cake, and pound cake. Aunt Nell, Daddy's sister, always brought banana pudding. And, of course, there were plates piled high with barbecue browned to a golden hue.

In a tin tub near the horse trough watermelons chilled for the afternoon.

Lossie and Flossie stood by the tables waving sticks with shredded newspaper tacked on the ends to shoo flies away.

After everyone had eaten, Mamma passed out little American flags to the children, and we marched around the yard waving them. Mamma's laughter was young and free, even with Daddy around.

Everywhere I looked were kinfolk—aunts, uncles, grand-parents, and cousins of every age. One of the uncles *got my nose* between his thumb and forefinger and then gave it back. I made sure I didn't get close to him again.

Younger adults pitched horseshoes, clanging metal against metal. The older folk rocked on the porch or sat un-der the shade trees.

Aunt Bernelle was telling a story I wanted to hear. It was about the first time she saw Uncle Rob. "He had on a blue bathing suit that matched his eyes," she said, "and I thought he was the best looking thing I'd ever seen in my life."

I had never before heard an adult talk about loving their husband or wife. I longed for Mamma and Daddy to do that. Mamma had gone to high school with Aunt Bernelle. They played basketball together. Aunt Bernelle and Uncle Rob had only one child, who died just after he was born.

Aunt Bernelle finished her story and hopped up. "All right," she called, "I'm a wild horse, and I'm going to catch all the boys and girls and take them home with me."

We ran squealing around her, staying just out of reach. The food in my stomach was beginning to slosh like butter-milk in a churn, when an older cousin slipped up behind and caught me under my arms. Lifting me, she twirled round and round. My feet sailed just above the ground. Finally, too dizzy to remain upright, she plopped on the ground still holding on to me. As trees above me spun in a sickening circle, I caught sight of Aunt Bernelle returning to the adults.

When I could stand, I started inside. Before passing through the first grouping of grown-ups, I was pulled down to sit on somebody's lap. The talk had turned to the Depression by the time I felt I could get away.

The boys were gathered in Guy's room around our cousin Lithco.

"Did you see her? Lithco asked as he bent over double in laughter, holding our black clothes brush in his hand. "She thought this was a cat."

Just then I noticed our cousin Evelyn, sitting by herself in the kitchen. Evelyn was a quiet girl and older than Guy. All of us knew she had a fear of cats, and Lithco had tricked her into thinking the hairs on the brush was the fur of a cat.

Seeing me, Evelyn smiled. "Do you want me to fix your nails?" she asked.

I nodded, and she opened a little bag she carried and took out a small pair of scissors and an emery stick. While she worked on my nails, trimming them, smoothing the edges, and shining them with a soft little buffer, I pretended I was a rich lady who was paying someone to give me a manicure.

The house was quiet when Evelyn finished my nails, and we went outside where the grown-ups still laughed and talked. I had forgotten all about Lithco and his prank.

Suddenly, a cousin yelled, "Hey, can we go to the barn?" Guy led the way.

My happiness was growing bit by bit that day, like the pieces of a puzzle falling into place, as we raced down that country road. We watched our city cousins marvel at the animals, played hide-and-seek in the corncrib, and jumped wildly in the itchy hay.

Finally, Guy herded us toward the pasture stream. We cupped our hands and drank from the bubbling spring. Those wearing shoes pulled them off to wade, and we splashed soothing water on our arms and legs, still stinging from the hay.

The sun was heading down toward the edge of the world when Aunt Nell called. "Lith–co–o–o!" Her voice sounded again and again through the pasture. We started back, reluctantly—wishing the day didn't have to end.

Guy, Louise, and I watched in silence as the cars chugged up the road. With each one, my happiness melted away.

# ~42~
# Fourth Grade

At last I was in Miss Harriet's class! Even knowing I'd have to master long division did not upset me. Miss Harriet was everything Guy and Louise had said and more. She loved us.

When Miss Harriet saw we were tired of sitting, she led us in exercises in the classroom. Sometimes after working hard in mathematics, she said, "Stand up and let's sing."

To our surprise, Miss Harriet wanted to hear what we were thinking. Did we agree with this—or that? Why or why not?

She got us so excited about learning we all wanted to talk at once. As a result, she had to get serious. "Raise your hand and get permission before you speak," she said. The name of any student speaking without permission was written on the chalkboard. A second offense brought a mark by the name, and that meant staying in five minutes of recess. One day Joe said, "Miss Harriet, please put a mark by my name. I want to stay in with you."

Miss Harriet loved geography, and she made us love it

too. We drew maps of places over the world and had contests to see who could color them the neatest.

While some children on the playground played rough games like Red Rover and Pop the Whip, Miss Harriet's boys played baseball, and her girls jumped rope.

When Miss Harriett was not watching the boys and cheering them on, she jumped rope with us girls. With *turners* whipping dust, we jumped and chanted:

*I had a letter from Nellie,*
*And what do you think she said?*
*Nellie had a baby, and his hair is red.*
*Now how many hairs are on his head?*
*One. Two. Three. Four. Five. . . .*

The rhyming gave us poetry, and with each verse, the rope lifted higher and higher and whipped faster and faster.

On special holidays Miss Harriett walked us across the highway and the railroad tracks to the house where she lived with her parents, and we had a party.

Reading on my own had become an important part of my life. *Heidi* was a favorite. Heidi and her grandfather, along with mountain air and goat's milk, helped make Clara well. Another book I read again and again was *Hans Brinker.* I could picture him skating on the canals in Holland.

Fourth grade was also the year of first haircuts for Louise and me. In late spring Mamma took us to Mr. Long's barbershop behind the bank. The smell of shaving lotions mixed with that of cigarettes in his small shop. We took a seat on chairs against the wall to wait our turn. A fan whirled like an airplane propeller in squeaks above our heads.

We watched Mr. Long shave a man sitting in his barber chair. Draped in a white robe, the man sat facing the big mirror. Mr. Long gripped the handle of a long, straight razor and slapped it back and forth on a leather strap hanging beneath the mirror. Then he held the razor in the air while he pumped the chair up with his foot and leaned the barber chair back.

The customer shut his eyes. Mr. Long picked up a mug filled with white cream and brushed it over the man's face and neck. I edged up close to Mamma. What if he cut him with the sharp razor?

Louise sat on the edge of her chair watching. Though we had seen Daddy shave, we had never seen anyone shaved in the barbershop.

Finally the shave was over. Mr. Long untied the string at the man's neck, loosening the white robe, and, like a magician performing a trick, spirited it to the side and flapped it in the air. Short pieces of hair drifted down.

In answer to "Next," Louise dashed over and climbed onto a board laid across the chair arms. Taking instructions from Mamma, Mr. Long cut Louise's long curls so the tips of her ears showed.

"It'll save me a lot of time in curling hair," Mamma told him. Each morning Mamma turned sections of our hair around a damped comb, forming long, sausage-shaped ringlets down our backs. Since our hair had natural curl, the ringlets stayed in place thoughout the day.

I watched Louise's hair fall over the white robe and onto the floor. She had a big smile on her face. Her hair was curlier than mine and, as Mr. Long cut, it twisted into little ringlets around her face.

Before I was ready, my turn came. Mr. Long wound the

string of the robe around my neck twice before he tied it. It felt awfully tight. The scissors clicked around my ears. I dared not speak or move.

When he finished, he turned the chair, and I saw myself in the mirror. My hair was straight. He'd cut away all my curls. Two more customers had come into the shop and taken seats. I didn't want them to look at me. I slid down from the chair and, stepping over my curls on the floor, hurried to Mamma and snuggled against her.

She thanked Mr. Long, paid him two quarters for our haircuts, and drove us to Grandma's.

In her kitchen Grandma looked up from the peas she was shelling. "Louise looks pretty good," she said, "but you have ruined poor little Idella."

# ~43~
# Electricity

At home I stood before the mirror and combed through my hair—something I'd not been able to do without wincing from tangles. Lossie watched me.

"What for you want to go and get your hair cut?" she asked.

Before I could answer, Louise bounced into the room. "We're going to get electric lights," she said. "Some men are putting up poles at the top of the hill."

Was she joking? I ran outside, with Lossie close behind. Two trucks were parked up the road. One had REA painted on the side. The other, a flat-bed truck, was loaded with long creosote-treated poles. Out in the field a yellow machine lifted a tall pole and placed it in a hole.

"Are we really getting electric lights?" I asked Mamma, who had come outside to look too.

Without turning her gaze from the workers, she answered, "Yes. Electricity is finally getting to the rural areas for farm families."

"What's REA?" I wanted to know.

"Rural Electrification Administration," Mamma answered absently.

It was true! I couldn't believe it. I was reading Nancy Drew books now, and kerosene lamps were hard to read by.

Before long, we actually had lights in every room of the house. In the center of each room, a bulb hung on a long cord from the ceiling. An attached string allowed us to pull the light on and off.

To our surprise, Daddy bought a radio. It was an Atwater Kent floor model. When static was not too bad, we could hear voices from faraway places. Mamma liked to listen to the news from broadcasters like H. V. Kaltenborn, Lowell Thomas, and Walter Winchell.

During the day the radio continued to crackle and grate with interference so that it was hard to make out words, but in evenings the reception was better.

Friday night was our favorite listening time. Sometimes the Boatwrights came down and laughed with us over the *Amos 'n' Andy* show. The characters were always getting into hilarious predicaments.

It was on the radio that I heard of the birth of the Dionne quintuplets in Ontario, Canada. They were the first quintuplets to live. Later, I saw the five little girls on the newsreel in the picture show and started keeping a scrapbook with pictures of Cecile, Annette, Marie, Yvonne, and Emily.

Electricity made life exciting. We were all enjoying our new pleasure when Aunt Maggie became very ill. Mamma went to be with her, and Guy, Louise, and I went to stay with Grandma. It was the first time I had ever been away from Mamma. From Grandma's house we could walk to school, but I felt all empty inside with Mamma gone. She had been away almost a week when Aunt Maggie died.

# ~44~
# Changes

With Aunt Maggie gone, Uncle Oscar decided to "break up housekeeping," as older people called giving up their homes and furnishings. He would retire from his job, sell his house, and take turns living with his sisters and younger brother, Rob, who also lived in Columbia.

Feeling closest to Mamma, because she lived with him and Aunt Maggie after her mamma died, he came to our house first. I was glad. Looking like the perfect gentleman in his dress suit, starched detachable collar, and polished shoes, he seemed out of place on our farm. As far as Daddy was concerned, he was.

Having ridden streetcars in Columbia, Uncle Oscar, like most city folks, did not own a car. Once, when he was driving our Model A from church after he had practiced a duet with Miss Katie for the following Sunday, another car rammed into the back of him.

"Didn't you put out your hand when you started to turn off the highway?" Daddy asked—as cars then had no turn signals.

"How could I?" Uncle Oscar replied in his dignified way. "The window was up."

"Awh, what difference does it make?" Mamma chimed. "The car'll still run."

Mamma was proud of "Buddy," the name she called Uncle Oscar, who was more like a father to her than a brother. He had made a good life for himself and Maggie, and they had shared that life with her. Mamma was always bragging on "Buddy's" rich tenor voice.

As he sat one day in his usual dreamy state, which Daddy called laziness, Uncle Oscar said, "Grace, I know Maggie would want you to have the dining room suit. You like having company." He looked about him at our small sitting area. "But where would you put it?"

Mamma smiled. "Maybe we can make room."

The next thing we knew, Mamma had a plan drawn up for two rooms to be added to our house, a bigger parlor and a dining room with French doors between. Even more surprising, her plan would turn the front of our house in a different direction, putting the front porch on the side of the house and nearer the road.

Though a new house was exciting, the idea took some getting used to. I liked our banistered porch just where it was. I liked to sit in the swing or a rocker and read. I thought of the time I was reading Helen Keller's life story. I closed my eyes, and kept them closed long after I wanted to see again. Birds warbled. Chickens clucked. From the pasture a mule brayed and a cow lowed. A breeze brought smells from sun-parched cornfields. From behind me in the house Mamma started singing. What if I couldn't open my eyes and see again? I had never forgotten the feeling.

I was still brooding over losing the old porch when Mamma announced her plan to Daddy. "You go on back to your highway job," she told him. "I can take care of everything."

But Daddy stayed home long enough to have poplar trees cut from our land and hauled to the lumber mill to be planed into boards. By the time building began, though, Daddy had returned to his job, and Uncle Oscar had gone to Aunt Alice's.

True to her word, Mamma took charge of the workmen and finally our parlor and dining room with fireplaces were ready. Uncle Oscar sent their mahogany table and chairs, buffet, and china cabinet, with its set of fragile Noritake china. He also sent an Oriental rug for the parlor. Best of all, he gave us his Edison phonograph.

The thick records, like "When Irish Eyes Are Smiling," became my dreaming music. I felt sure the one called "When You and I Were Young Maggie" had been written about the way Uncle Oscar talked to Aunt Maggie.

Sometimes I waltzed about on the rug as I listened. When the music started slowing to its death, I'd waltz by and give the phonograph another wind. Other times I spread Mamma's old sheet music, that I'd found in a buffet drawer, on the table and pretended I was a concert pianist, moving my fingers over imaginary keys as the Edison played.

My favorite piece of sheet music was "Loves Golden Star." On the front was a drawing of a girl with flowers in her hair. Behind her was a bright star with hearts at each point.

The piece had no lyrics, just music symbols. Beneath the title was the word "Reverie." When I checked our dictionary for the meaning, I was surprised to read "daydreaming"—my favorite thing to do.

Only one of our new possessions bothered me. Over the dining room fireplace hung a large painting called "The Tree of Life." It reminded me of the death certificate of my grandmother, Idella Fallaw. In the painting was a tree with angels hovering about it. Golden light flooded through the tree's branches where words like "knowledge" and "obedience" rested.

I knew the picture represented the fall of man and the banishment of Adam and Eve from the Garden of Eden. Still, it made me feel uncomfortable. And as we sat around the table studying in the evenings, it always drew my eyes.

At last Mamma could entertain the way she wanted. With the table stretched to its limit—all the leaves in place— she would cover the top with white damask cloth and set it with Aunt Maggie's daintily flowered china.

With the dining room set for guests, the mirrored buffet reflected macaroni pie, sweet potato soufflé, ham, baked chicken and pan dressing, rice and giblet gravy, fresh vegetables from the garden or canned ones from the pantry, and pies and cakes.

"I can be a lady as well as anybody," Mamma said as she and Floride put the finishing touches on her meal. "That was how Maggie brought me up."

One of our earliest guests in the new dining room was a missionary visiting our church. The evening she came Louise wore her "boy pants." The missionary looked at Louise with a frown and said, "If God had intended you to be a boy, he would have made you one."

Mamma gave Louise a "keep quiet" look and changed the subject. Mamma didn't see anything wrong with girls wearing pants around the house. Even Miss Katie, my Sunbeam teacher, had on overalls the day our class went to see her farm animals.

A tea set painted with geisha girls in Japanese scenes sat on top of the china closet. On dreary winter days Mamma would take it down, and we'd sip hot chocolate from the tiny cups. On the saucers and sides of the cups Japanese girls paraded over bridges or strolled among peach-colored blossoms. Some twirled gilded umbrellas.

When Uncle Oscar returned for his "stay" with us, he was pleased that we were enjoying the possessions he had passed along. . . . We would continue to enjoy them for many years.

# ~45~
# The Macks

With a silver table knife, Uncle Newlin stirred a quart jar of homemade peanut butter to mix in the oil settled on top. We were at the dining room table finishing up our noon meal—which we called dinner—at our Mack relatives in Gaston. Peanut butter stirred into syrup and spread on homemade biscuits would be our dessert.

Uncle Newlin had been in the Navy in World War I. A large photograph of him in his uniform hung over the mantel in the dining room. Since he was a rural mail carrier, the

Depression had not been as hard on the Macks as it had on others. Though Uncle Newlin owned many acres of land, he didn't depend on farming for the livelihood of his family. Food always seemed plentiful when all ten of us children gathered around the table.

As he stirred, Uncle Newlin spoke in his deadpan drawl about his early years of delivering mail through the country. We had been taught to keep quiet when adults spoke, so we listened to Uncle Newlin's story.

"When I first started carrying the mail," he began, "I rode horseback. It took me six hours to go twenty-five miles. People on my route didn't get newspapers or have radios. They counted on me to tell them what was going on and how the other folks along the route were getting along. I bought a used car in 1918 but it wasn't dependable, so four years later I got a new Ford for $500."

In spite of his expressionless way of speaking, Uncle Newlin had a sense of humor—or so Mamma thought. One day he took her out to see a cow he'd named for her. I didn't think it was funny to hear him call "Gra–ace" and see the cow amble toward us. But Mamma laughed.

Mamma had a great sense of humor. When she was in a good mood, her laughter echoed around us.

After we finished the dessert, we were allowed to leave the table.

As we cousins were playing outside later, Bryce excited us with an announcement. "I'm starting a club. Anybody who can find the top of a 666 tin can be a member. That's your pass."

We headed toward the trash pile back near the woods to search for the little red and yellow discarded tins that had once held salve. Every family used the ointment for bites, scrapes, and a variety of other skin problems.

"Now," Bryce said when our 666 tops admitted us to the upstairs room over their garage, "you have to be initiated."

From the earliest age Bryce had been curious about how things worked. Now as a young teen he spent his money on books about electricity. Somehow he'd managed to get an old wall telephone. It no longer worked as a phone, but he had fun with it in other ways.

"All right," he told us, "get in a circle and hold hands."

When the younger boys made faces at holding girls' hands, Bryce said, "Of course, if you don't want to be a member, you don't have to; but you have to leave right now. The initiation is secret."

The boys didn't look too happy, but they stayed. Bryce broke into the circle where Robert and Louise held hands. "You two won't hold hands," he said. "You'll hold these wires." He held out small wires connected to the telephone. "And don't turn them loose, no matter what, until I tell you. Anybody who stops holding hands before I give the signal, will not be accepted into the club."

The room was quiet when Bryce stepped to the little crank on the side of the phone. He cranked, and Louise let out a faint squeal that rippled around the circle.

When the strange tingling ran in my hand, up my arm, through my body, and out the other arm to the cousin beside me, I found out the reason for the squeal. Still, nobody let go but held on tighter as the mild volt of electricity ran around and around in a circle through our bodies. Then just as suddenly as it began, it stopped.

Bryce seemed proud of himself. "You are now members

of the 666 Club," he announced.

He was no prouder than I felt or the others looked. Bravery, it seemed, had made us real members.

Bryce's inventions kept us entertained. As members of the club, we got to ride on an old car Bryce pieced together from wrecked ones. This one didn't have a roof. We all piled into the car and jiggled down the clay road to the mill pond to swim.

After supper, we read. Each of us pulled down a volume from a set called *The Book of Knowledge*. When somebody let out a giggle or a whistle, someone else said, "I want that one after you." And another said, "Then me." My favorite was the one with Greek myths.

One evening Uncle Newlin paid us five cents a quart to shell butter beans for canning. The grown-ups put the beans into glass jars for storage. The following night loud bangs like gunshots sounded from the cellar. One by one the tops of the canned jars blew off. As far as I know, nobody ever learned why.

# ~46~
# Aunt Alice

When it came time for us to return home from Gaston, I begged Mamma to go by Aunt Alice's. "Please! I want her to go home with us."

For a wonder, Mamma agreed.

Aunt Alice was Mamma's sister, thirteen years older, who gave the good hugs. When we asked her to come with us, she held her mouth in that odd way she did when she told stories. "Go ask Elliott if he'll come for me," she said.

I didn't know any families that had more than one car. And, Aunt Alice couldn't drive. In fact, few women did. Most depended on their husbands to take them places. But not Mamma. "I can drive anything with a steering wheel on it," she boasted.

"My gosh!" Uncle Elliott, a tall, thin southern gentleman, looked up in amazement as we ran toward the chinaberry tree where he'd taken refuge from the summer heat. "Somebody left the barn door open."

In answer to our begging for Aunt Alice to go home with us, he said, "Well, I guess so. When I can't get along without her any longer, I'll come get her."

We raced back to deliver the good news.

On the ride home I had to sit between Guy and Louise to keep them from fighting. Wind whished in the windows, making it hard for me to hear what Mamma and Aunt Alice were talking about. I perched on the edge of the seat to listen. Aunt Alice was saying, "You know Buddy has his own room at Rob's."

Uncle Rob was two years older than Mamma. His wife, Aunt Bernelle, was the one who played "horse" with us on the Fourth of July. I thought how quiet it must be at Aunt Bernelle's house and at Aunt Alice's without children.

Behind my back, Guy and Louise argued over a game of cow poker. "You didn't have time to count that many cows," Guy accused.

"If there are too many to count, you're supposed to estimate and say twenty-five." Louise made up her own rules when she played games.

"You can take my side, Idella," Guy said. "Louise is not playing fair."

"You're just a sore loser." Louise flung her words at him. "And you know we're coming to a cemetery on your side and you'll have to bury your cows."

I didn't want to play cow poker. Instead, I pulled up closer behind Mamma. "How much longer?" I asked. I was thirsty, and my hair was blowing in my eyes and mouth. I wanted to get home so I could hear what Aunt Alice was telling. I loved sitting with her on our new porch, which I had come to like almost as much as the old one, even if it didn't have banisters. I liked to listen to Aunt Alice talk and then turn her words over in my mind. Sometimes after supper she sat on the porch and rubbed lemon peel from her ice tea on her face. She said it kept her complexion fair. Everybody said Louise had her coloring. In spite of her large size, Aunt Alice was a pretty, graceful lady.

We learned lots of things from Aunt Alice. Once she walked to the edge of the pasture, took a twig from a sassafras tree and showed us how old-time people frayed the ends and used it as a toothbrush. The tang of the sassafras together with Aunt Alice's perfumed powder produced a strange aroma.

In the afternoons Aunt Alice slipped out of her starched dress and lay down for a rest. Like Grandma, she never removed her corset except at night. Aunt Alice's body rose like a little mountain from the bed, and Louise and I couldn't resist. In spite of Mamma's warning to "Stop pestering Alice," we took turns climbing on top of the "hill" and falling, exclaiming, "Rolling down the mountain." Aunt Alice laughed with us.

When we had company, Mamma had the evening meal in our new dining room with our white damask tablecloth. We always lingered at the table waiting for stories when Aunt Alice visited. With a little coaxing from Louise, they came.

"Aunt Alice," Louise asked, "did they ever find the man who stuck his hand in the woman's bedroom window?"

"You know," she answered in her most serious tone, "they never did."

"Will you tell us about it again?" I asked.

Aunt Alice scooted her plate back and crossed her arms on the table edge. Her voice took on that mysterious lilt. "It was on a hot day in summer—just like this one—when you had to put the windows up to breathe. Well, this lady named Abigail pushed the head of her bed right up to her window so she could feel any breeze that happened to come along. Then she blew out her lamp and stretched out on her bed with her head right up to the window screen."

Aunt Alice paused, then picked up the story again, her voice lowered. When Abigail fell asleep, somebody slipped up to her window and quietly slit the screen. Then he reached his arm through that opening and held a handkerchief soaked with chloroform over her mouth and nose."

"Did it kill her?" Guy asked as if he didn't remember.

"No, she didn't die, but she didn't know she was in the world until on up in the next day. And while she was dead to the world, robbers came in her house—in the very room where she was—and stole every blessed thing they could carry away."

I loved Aunt Alice's stories. My stomach tightened with fear while my mind pulled at the words, willing them to come out until bit by bit the ending emerged. I felt all shivery, especially now that it was growing dark outside. I thought of the man yelling so long ago at night in our pasture.

"We don't have robbers around here," I said and looked at Mamma to confirm it.

Before she could, Aunt Alice reached out and took my hand. She turned the palm up and traced the line running all the way across it. "This means you are going to live a long, long time," she said as if her knowledge came from some place far off. She traced another line before she added, "And one day you will be a school teacher." She smiled and folded my fingers over, as if her fortune was a secret I must keep forever.

She told Guy that he would make lots of money and Louise that wherever she went she would make people laugh and be happy.

"How did you learn to tell fortunes?" I asked.

"I learned from a lady who calls herself Sister Mary," she said. "She lives on the road to Columbia. I was so upset when I lost my amethyst brooch Elliot gave me that I went to see her. She told me to look in the back closet on my paisley voile dress. Lo and behold! There it was." She looked at Mamma and winked before she added, "I watched how she told things, and I do it just the way she did." Suddenly she pushed back her chair. "But right now I need to help Grace with these dishes."

Mamma got up from the table. "The dishes are going to sit in the dishpan until Floride comes in the morning. Besides, I want to show you my crocheting."

Later on as we sat still enjoying our new electric lights, Mamma started telling Aunt Alice about Daddy going back to the highway department. All of a sudden she said, "The children can tell you which one of us they love the most."

"Oh, Grace," Aunt Alice scolded, "don't ask them that."

My insides felt all hollow. I missed Daddy. After I went to bed, I thought about what Mamma had said. Sometimes I didn't understand her. I was glad I didn't have to say which one I loved most, for I loved them both. I just wanted them to love each other.

# ~47~
# The Brooder House

Guy's way of making money each spring was raising chickens. When the biddies came in at the feed store, he bought twenty-four—just the number to fit in his little tin brooder. Now that we had electricity, he no longer used a lantern to keep them warm. Instead, he put a light bulb inside a tin shield so the chicks wouldn't get burned when they hovered around it.

Each day he fed and watered them and put clean paper on the rack under the wire floor.

"Won't you let me hold just one?" I sat watching the chirping little balls of yellow fluff.

"Nope. It might get sick, and then they'd all get sick and die."

"I never get to hold any biddies," I complained to Mamma. "The hens won't let me near theirs, and Guy won't either."

I thought of the time a setting hen was off her nest and I climbed up in the chicken coop to look at the eggs. Some of the shells had cracked. As I watched, a wet little chick pecked his way out. I'd never forgotten it.

On his next trip home, Daddy said, "I'm staying here through spring. The place needs me. Besides, I'm thinking about starting a brooder house."

It was 1935, and the worst of the Depression seemed to be behind us. Daddy and Pete built a brooder house at the upper edge of our backyard. A brickmason added a kind of heating unit to protect the newborn chicks from the chill of spring nights.

When hundreds of soft little chicks arrived in their cardboard boxes, we introduced them to their new home. With a caution from Mamma to move slowly so as not to frighten them, I helped with their care. I filled food trays with mash and water jars with fresh well water. I liked screwing on the jar caps with their tin circles. When the jars were turned upside down, the chicks could drink from the tin circle. The eager little biddies dipped their beaks for a drink and then tilted heads back so the water could run down their throats.

Some days their drinking water ran red with medicine, added to keep them from getting *sore head*.

Every day after school I rushed to the brooder house and lost myself in a golden world of cheeping little chicks. My longing to hold biddies was fulfilled.

On the night before Easter a terrible thing happened. I was awakened by frantic, shouting voices. Louise was not in our bed. I ran to the kitchen where the light was on. Louise stood in the open doorway. Beyond her, I could see the brooder house engulfed in flames.

Daddy and Pete struggled to push back the flaming wall with long boards. Fire licked and crackled around them. Guy jerked frantically on the well chain, bringing up water as fast as he could. Mamma dashed back and forth, madly sloshing water around the area burning closest to our house. The blaze roared and the crackling sound grew louder and louder. Shouts of the fire fighters were lost in the popping fire.

The biddies had perished, the brooder house destroyed. Now the fight was on to keep the twisting, flaring flames away from our house. Sparks swept up into the night and fell back into the shadows.

"Get the children out of the house!" Daddy yelled.

"Go out the front door!" Mamma screamed as she dashed by us with her buckets.

I followed Louise. We ran barefoot up the slope by the apple tree and stood shivering in our nightgowns. I saw a bright orange sheet of fire travel up the hill, billowing smoke into the dark sky. Daddy and Pete had managed to push the fiery walls up the slope and away from our house.

For the first time I realized I was standing in my garden by my dusty millers and my face was wet with tears.

# ~48~
# Asparagus Season

Smoldering ash and the charred smell were painful reminders of our burned brooder house. I ached for the perished biddies.

"Thank goodness we are all right," Mamma said, "and our house was spared."

The searing heat had singed Daddy's and Pete's eyelashes and blistered their faces and hands, but, as Mamma said, we had much to be thankful for.

The main problem now was money. Everything had been put into the raising of chickens to sell in several months as broilers. That expected income was gone. Food was still plentiful on the farm, but cash was needed. We now had an electric bill to pay. One month, only Guy had the eleven dollars to meet that payment.

Guy would be going into seventh grade when school started the next year, and he was becoming more serious about life. He had recently joined the church and begun to think of things in terms of *right* and *wrong*.

"Mamma," I heard him say once, "a boy at school was baptized when I was, but he said a cuss word today."

Playing "for keeps" in the game of marbles concerned him. Was that gambling? he wondered. He took a poll of teachers at school to see what they thought.

Pete plowed the field for Guy's peanuts and helped him get the plants in the ground.

I began to worry that Daddy would have to go back to the highway job, but he soon made an announcement that lifted my spirits. "I've decided to weed and fertilize the asparagus fields. They've been allowed to grow wild too long."

To my surprise, Mamma went along with his plan. "The market's got to be better this year," she said. I figured she was thinking of how the asparagus shed came to life with people laughing and talking as they packed the green shoots for shipping.

The world that seemed to come to a stop for me when the brooder house burned, moved on.

That spring was the first time I ever saw Daddy plow.

After school I carried water to him and Pete where they pre-pared the asparagus fields. Daddy gripped the plow handles in his struggle with the mule. He was hot and frustrated. He swore at his plow blade for popping out of the ground and skittering along.

Several rows over, Pete's hands hung loose on the plow handles, the lines to the mule looped over his wrist. With a "Gee" here and a "Haw" there, he moved his flubbering mule along. I could hear him muttering. "You ain't got to act so dumb just cause you a mule. I done warn you 'bout putting your big feets on the furrows."

Plow blades turned up the plague of southern farmers: wire grass. The grass was then raked and burned on the ter-races—a hard, hot job.

I liked the fields. I liked the smell of the turned earth. I wanted to stay and watch, but Daddy had other ideas. "Go on back to the house and get out of this sun," he told me. "Af-ter a while you can bring us some more water."

Before we knew it, the points of young asparagus stems broke through the earth. Workers were happy to come to the farm to pack asparagus.

Pete brought the crop in from the fields on a slide made from two slender tree trunks with boards nailed aross them. On Saturdays we got to ride with him. "Keep your feets up," he cautioned.

Guy added, "And be quiet." Guy held the reins of the mule while Pete sat on the front edge and cut the green stalks at ground level just before the slide passed over them.

"I judge if the slide gone hit de top of de stalk," Pete said. "Dat way I know it ready."

Pete was proud of his fast harvesting. Only rarely did he

have to ask Guy to hold back on the reins. When Guy did, the mule whinnied, showing his yellow teeth.

I couldn't wait to get home from school to listen to the shed workers talk. Some graded the asparagus according to size. Others stacked the gritty stalks, still damp from the harvest, into metal holders. Once a holder was filled, workers clamped the top down, tied red ribbons around the top and bottom of the bunch, and sliced the ends to an even length. On and on they talked and bunched. Finally, the green asparagus with red ribbons made a pretty picture standing upright on the damp moss of shipping crates.

Sometimes I'd climb stairs to the shed's second level where our sugarcane syrup was stored. Crystals of syrup stuck around the tops of the gallon jars. I broke away pieces and sucked them like hard candy. Sounds from below floated up to me: the clank of the metal bunchers, the *slice-chop* of sharp knives against the tables, good-natured talking. Sitting up there listening, I created a private little place all my own.

When the packing day was over, I rode to the depot with Daddy to put the crates on the train to be shipped to market.

The only unpleasant part of the whole season was the smell of asparagus cooking. Mamma served it every day. If asparagus smelled that bad, I figured, it must taste awful. I refused even to try it.

# ~49~
# Bad News

Lightning struck a big oak near the barn. The gigantic tree trunk splintered, toppling onto the fence.

"A bad sign. Dat what it is." Pete worked at mending the fence to keep the animals in.

I went up to the house and told Mamma what he'd said.

"Awh, don't put any sway in that kind of talk." She shook her head. "Most of the colored folks are superstitious."

But still I worried. What bad thing might happen?

It was not unusual for Ranger to crawl way back under the low part of our house. He liked the bed he made for himself the winter Aunt Betty lived with us. But when Mamma came to pick us up from school, she seemed concerned.

"Ranger's been under the house all day," she said. "I know it's cooler there, but with the weather this nice, I can't understand it. He didn't even come to eat when I called him."

"Maybe he stuck his nose in an ant bed," Louise offered. "He did that the other day."

"Or he's pouting because he let my rooster get the best of him," Guy said.

"Could be," Mamma mused.

We spent the rest of the afternoon taking turns coaxing Ranger out. We sweet-talked him every way possible.

Mamma fixed him a bowl of grits with meat scraps. Though she always said things like "For heaven's sake, Ranger, move. You almost knocked me off balance." or "Put that dog outside," we knew she loved him too.

Guy tied a piece of pork on a long stick and dangled it back to him. He didn't move or make a sound.

When Pete came up to the house and heard about it, he said, "Poison dogs don't eat. Plenty people scared of Ranger. Somebody may done poison him."

I saw Mamma frown at Pete. "Oh, I don't think anybody would do a thing like that."

"A snake could have bitten him," Daddy said later on.

Still we continued to call and talk to him. That night we reminded each other to put Ranger in our prayers.

The next morning he still had not come out.

That afternoon I could tell by Mamma's face the news was bad. Ranger was dead.

"Your daddy and Pete buried him out by the walnut tree," she told us. "We'll go to the spring and dig up some violets for his grave."

It was the quietest ride from school we'd ever had. I knew if I tried to speak, I would burst into tears.

At home, nobody was hungry for a change. We headed for Ranger's grave. The mound of earth was still fresh.

It was a sad procession down the sloping pasture to the stream Ranger loved. Only this time he was not there to plop his big feet in the water and splash it into silver droplets.

Using slivers of mica from the bank, we scooped up violets and headed toward home and Ranger's grave. Flossie and Lossie came and stood with us. Mamma talked about how God loved Ranger too. She said a prayer, and we planted the violets. Then Guy went under the shed to make a marker for his grave.

Our usual excitement didn't accompany school closing

for the summer that year. We had all looked forward to spending more time with Ranger. Now he was gone. I felt so sad I thought my heart would break.

# ~50~
# Typhoid Fever

"Bad things happen in threes," Grandma always said. She was right that year. The brooder house burned and Ranger died. Then all of our hogs became sick with cholera. Within a week they were dead. Only Porky, who had never lived in the barnyard, survived.

We heard the same terrible news from other farms. Our slow recovery from the Depression suffered a startling setback. Once again, Daddy contacted Mr. Hook and went back to work with the highway department.

In a matter of days word circulated that cases of typhoid fever were being reported. This serious disease, with high fever and weakness, and, in severe cases, death, moved into our town. Lakes, picture shows, and other public places where people gathered closed. Typhoid fever was highly contagious.

A public health station was set up in the colored school to give vaccinations to protect those not already exposed. We had no choice but to take the series of three shots. Even the vaccine made us feverish.

One morning Pete did not come up to the house. "Miss Grace," Flossie called from outside the back door, "Daddy's sick."

Mamma went home with Flossie. In a short while she

was back. "I'm going for the doctor," she said, "Pete's burning up with fever."

The doctor did not follow Mamma down the country road the way he had when the snake bit Guy. Mamma's voice shook when she said, "He says there's nothing he can do. He's telling the sick to drink water and try to keep the fever down." *Pete had typhoid fever.*

Mamma gathered clean cloths and the aspirin bottle and started out the door. Then she turned back to us. "I'll send the girls up here. They ought not to be around their daddy."

Later that day Lossie and Flossie's aunt came for them.

For weeks Mamma took care of Pete. She took him food and fed it to him when he was too sick to feed himself. She would never let us go inside his house, but one day as I stood waiting, I heard Pete's weak voice say, "You a angel, Miss Grace. You a angel."

At night I prayed in earnest. If Lossie and Flossie could get typhoid fever from their father, why wouldn't Mamma?

One night Louise woke with a start. In a cry as sharp as thorns, she screamed, "Mamma! Pete's at the foot of my bed!"

"It's all right, Weezie." I heard Mamma hurrying to comfort her. "You were just dreaming."

At daylight, Mamma found Pete dead. We believed Louise had seen a wraith, a premonition of his death.

Years later we heard that Flossie had been scrubbing her aunt's floor with lye soap when some of the water splashed in her face, damaging her eyesight. I never saw her or my friend Lossie again.

# ~51~
# A Feeling of Loss

Pete's death left a vacant spot in our lives. Typhoid fever continued to rage. Another neighbor died. The air was thick with worry.

The empty tenant house was a sad reminder of Pete and my friendship with Lossie. Only the music of the Edison made me feel better.

Before summer came to an end, a couple with one son about Guy's age moved into Pete's house. Gillfish, as the boy was called, was the most daring person I have ever known. Louise's jumps from heights and Lithco's daring balancing act on the church balcony rails seemed mild compared to the way Gillfish acted. One day he swung so high in our rope swing, which hung from a backyard oak, the swing looped over the limb. Delighted with his feat, he kept trying to do it again.

Gillfish had a knowledge of many things new to us. He knew how to scrape smelly resin from the sweet gum tree, work the sticky substance into a ball, and chew it for gum. Even more important, he knew all about the *boogerman.*"

"You act ugly," he cautioned, "dat boogerman gone come whiles you sleeping and carve out yo gizzard."

"Mamma," I asked one night after I'd heard another of Gillfish's warnings about all the devil could do, "if I hang my hand off the bed, will anything get it?"

Her laughter answered, even before she said, "Who in the world would want your hand?"

Daddy did not try to raise pigs after the terrible plague so Gillfish's father did not come to the house for slop the way Pete had. But one day he came to ask Mamma if he could borrow a dollar until payday. I was waltzing around to the music of "Annie Laurie," playing on the Edison.

"You dance," he said to me, "you going to de debil for sure. Yes, Ma'am, he be already walking on yo grave."

Even our trip to Gaston, always a highlight of the summer, was a disappointment. A September gale blew in on the day we arrived. A cold rain drummed on the house and ran over the windows in gushes. We couldn't go swimming.

Because of the bad weather Uncle Newlin had stored cotton in a shed until he could get it to the gin. In spite of the rain, we dashed to the shed and played on the mountains of white fluff. We dug tunnels, breathing in the oily smell of the seeds.

During the night my cousin Robert suffered an asthma attack. We could hear him struggling to breathe. Aunt Frances stayed up with him all night. The next morning the sight of him lying against his pillows, wheezing and pale, made me forgive him for making mine and Margie's lives so miserable.

When we returned home, the family had moved from Pete's house. I was glad. Mamma located Gillfish's father on another farm and drove there to ask him what happened.

"Miss Grace," he said, "I can't live in no haunted house."

"Whatever would make you say such a thing?" Mamma asked in disbelief.

"You know dat bad rainstorm dat washed out de barn road whiles you was gone? Well, it cause a bloody spot to come up where Pete die. I can't live in dat house."

Later, Mamma went down to scrub the house. She did

not find a *spot*. For as long as the house stayed empty, we children and our cousins sneaked in with fear and trembling after hard rains. But we never did find the bloody spot Gillfish's daddy talked about.

In the long summer evenings on the porch, I watched for the beam of car lights bouncing down the road. Would Daddy ever come home?

# ~52~
# Growing Up

At last I was in the big building at school. Now when Mamma dropped us off in the mornings, all three of us marched up the high steps to the columned portico and through heavy glass-topped double doors. An oily smell still clung to the floor from the previous day's cleaning.

The sounds of the big, two-story building were different from the little four-room building in which I had spent the last four years. We no longer had a teacher ringing a handbell. Instead, an electric buzzer, just outside our fifth-grade room, blasted. All day the buzzer signaled the change of classes for high school students. The jarring ring never failed to make me jump. Moments after each buzz, feet clomped up and down the wooden staircase, and voices of older students echoed through the hallway.

Due to the repeated failure to pass from one grade to the next, some students in my class were older than those of us who had just moved up from fourth grade. In this way we had *inherited* Homer and his sister Sadie Mae. Both sat hunched over in their desks with scowling expressions. We all knew that the slightest remark on the school ground could spark vile language and a fistfight begun by Homer, with Sadie Mae joining in.

It was in the classroom, this particular year, that I experienced for the first time a young person defying adult authority. One day, when our teacher, Mrs. Gunter, stepped to the office just across the hall, Homer, barefoot and clad only in bib overalls caked with dried dirt, jumped up and locked the door behind her.

My longtime classmates and I sat stiff in fear, awaiting the outcome. At first Mrs. Gunter's expression through the glassed-top door appeared puzzled. Then it changed to a look of disbelief. To my knowledge, the door had never been locked.

Homer just sat hunched over his desk with a grin crooking the side of his mouth. His fingers, with their dirty nails, were laced together on his desk top. No student dared say anything or get up and open the door for fear Homer's, and maybe even Sadie Mae's, temper would erupt at them.

Mrs. Gunter, being the quiet disciplinarian she was, peered through the door at the class and obviously sized up the situation. In moments she had the principal, who, with what I supposed to be a skeleton key, unlocked the door.

I felt I was watching characters performing on a stage as the principal hauled off Homer, who was yelling, "Who cares? I don't give a hoot."

We sat quiet as Homer's voice faded down the hall and Mrs. Gunter regained her composure.

Rumor had it Homer was expelled. Soon, Sadie Me dropped out too. There was no law that children had to attend school, and as far as I know, Homer and Sadie Mae never returned.

From late fall until early spring heat rose from steel radiators beneath the classroom's long windows. Alternately the contraptions sighed and hissed. Occasionally they spit steam. In spite of the annoying noises, the radiators kept us toasty warm.

It was in this setting that I coped with Roman numerals and Mrs. Gunter instilled in me a love of history. She let us act out scenes from our books. We made up a play about the Lost Colony, an early settlement on Roanoke Island. Our history book said that when provisions grew short, John White sailed back to England for supplies. Upon his return, he discovered the colony had disappeared.

The class grieved with John White for his little granddaughter, Virginia Dare, the first child born in the settlement. Though a neighboring tribe of friendly Indians loved Virginia, calling her White Fawn, fierce Indians teamed against the little colony. Some people think these Indians took the little girl and made her a princess. No trace of her was ever found.

Still painfully shy, I had agonizing moments—like the time I wore new shoes to a birthday party. As I made my way across the room, the shoes squeaked. Somebody called out, "Idella's got on new shoes." I felt my face turn beet red. For the remainder of the party, I dared not get up for fear my shoes would squeak again. I was thankful there was no piano for the musical game of Upset the Fruit Basket.

Being in plays was different. When Mrs. Gunter gave me the part of Pocahontas, I was happy. In the play, my father, Chief Powhatan, was about to kill Captain John Smith, leader of the Jamestown settlement. John Smith—who was really Joe

Holstein—was lying on the floor and Powhatan stood over him with his tomahawk raised. I moved between the two to beg my father to spare Captain Smith's life. Classmates laughed at the scene, but I did not mind. I was no longer a shy girl. I was Pocahontas!

Even as the lowest grade in the big building, Mrs. Gunter's class shared the same recess as the older students. This school yard had a different look from the one next door at the four-room building. Kids didn't run around yelling and chasing each other. Except for some of the boys doing lay-ups on the outdoor basketball court, everybody just *hung around* and talked.

Some of the girls sat on the steps; others went out by the highway to perch on the curb. It was here that my girlfriends and I began to talk about "big girl" things like "who liked who."

The talk never got too serious until the day Ethelyn, with her beautiful copper-colored hair, came home from school with me. We sat on the edge of the yard near a clump of wild ragged robins.

"You know where babies come from, don't you?" she asked.

I don't remember if I answered her queston, but I would never have let her or anyone else know that at the age of ten I knew almost nothing about "the facts of life."

In those days having babies was never discussed, especially around children. Mothers-to-be did not even let it be known they were expecting a baby. People knew only when it became obvious. After that time, it wasn't considered "good taste" for a pregnant woman to appear in public.

Ethelyn proceeded to tell me what she knew. As she

spoke, my insides turned sour like a green apple. How did she know so much? Should I believe all she was saying?

I thought long and hard about my newfound knowledge. I was confused, but far too shy to ask her questions or tell a living soul what she had passed on to me.

# ~53~
# Topsy-turvy World

Daddy came home to stay. Mr. Hook had retired, and his crew disbanded. Things were not good on the farm. Mamma still had her garden for canning, but without hogs there would be no meat in the smokehouse. Pete's house lay empty and the land idle. Daddy sold the two riding horses he had surprised Guy with a few years before.

As I had always done, I took refuge in books, this time those by Louisa Mae Alcott. *Little Women* had the kind of family I wanted. Though Louise was more like Jo than I was, I determined to follow Jo's lead. Like she did in *Jo's Boys*, I vowed never to marry but to start a home for boys. I read *Eight Cousins* eagerly. It reminded me of my Gaston cousins.

I also loved poetry. I took Mamma's leather-bound copy of Robert Burns's poems, with its linen-like pages, for my own.

Each time I returned from the pages of books to the real world, I became more aware of the problems of the time. Families were finding it harder and harder to live off the land. Everybody we knew had money problems. Many families gave up—or lost—their homes and moved in with friends or relatives.

The start of a school year usually lifted my spirits. But even sixth grade was a letdown. We began the year with a substitute teacher, followed by others who stayed only a short time each.

One bright spot was the annual May Day celebration. That year girls my age would dance around the Maypole. Mamma made my dress, as other mothers did, by lapping crepe paper in the shape of tulip leaves over one another and fastening them onto a pink cloth bodice and skirt.

Later, in the Maypole dance, we would plait our streamers, moving to the music—weaving in and out, over and under, and around and around. Like real leaves, our crepe paper tulip leaves would rustle with our movements.

Each day, near the close of school, we walked behind our church to practice with our music teacher, Mrs. Truluck. While seniors glided, dipped, bowed, and curtsied in a minuet to the rhythm of the music on the record player, the rest of us sat around on the sloping grounds to wait our turns.

"I know something," a classmate said to me, "but I'm not supposed to tell."

"What?" She knew her comment would make me beg to find out.

"I said I wouldn't tell."

"Who told you?"

"I can't tell," she answered, pressing her lips together. With a sudden change of mind, she asked, "Promise you won't tell a soul I told you?"

I nodded.

"She said your daddy has a girlfriend."

The day was very hot, but her accusation slid like an icicle into my heart. When I was able to speak, I said, "Well, I don't care who told you; it's not so."

Mrs. Truluck's call for the Maypole dancers sounded as if it came from some faraway place. The joy of the dance was shattered.

Later at home I listened to Mamma and Daddy talk.

"I sure as shooting can't look for a job without a car," Daddy said. "And there's no work around Ridge Spring. That's a fact."

"And," Mamma shot back, "we can't stay in the country without a car."

Several weeks later, Grandma and Granddaddy moved from their home to a house near the cemetery. The new place was located on part of a large acreage where Granddaddy had grown up. It was still owned by a relative who wanted to plant wheat on the land and wanted Granddaddy to oversee the work. The move would leave my grandparents' home in town vacant. It was decided that our family and Clyde, Jr.'s, would move into the house.

Daddy sold the mules, Bittersweet and her calf, and Porky, who had grown into a full-sized hog.

"I'm taking the chickens," Mamma said. No one would have dared to disagree with her.

The gloom I felt must have shown on my face. "Don't look so sad," Mamma said. "We'll come back as soon as things get better. We're just closing up the house and taking only what we have room for."

Our beautiful dining room suit, the hot chocolate set, the Edison—all were being left behind.

My mind churned with worry. How did Guy and Louise feel? Had they heard what my classmate had told me? Questions I would not ask haunted me.

# ~54~
# A New Home

Throughout our move to Grandma's house, my feelings were all mixed up. On one hand, it would be exciting to live in town. We could walk to church and school. And, I knew I would enjoy living in the same house with my cousin, Clyde, Jr. Still, leaving the farm—if only temporarily—made my heart ache.

In the small hall just inside Grandma's front door were two other entrances: one opening into our side of the house, the other into Clyde, Jr.'s. That deep well I dreaded so much at the end of Grandma's long back porch was on our side of the house—just beyond the window where I would sleep.

I was eleven in that year of 1936 and "too old," according to adults, to play with dolls. Reluctantly, I left them and their shoe boxes of handmade clothes behind.

Daddy helped us settle in and then disappeared. No jobs were available nearby for men, but a new dressmaking industry in a neighboring town needed women. No women I knew worked outside the home, except school teachers, and most of them were not married. I didn't like it much when Mamma and Aunt Ruby took jobs. I missed having Mamma around all the time. The house seemed empty without her.

Since Guy was oldest, he was left in charge when Mamma and Aunt Ruby were working. That fall his duty was put to the test. In the middle of the afternoon the sky grew as dark as late evening. No storm seemed to be brewing. No smell of rain hung in the air. We didn't know what to make of it.

Suddenly a great spear of green lanced the sky. Frosty white beams began to play over the red clouds.

"It must be the end of the world," Guy told Louise, Clyde, Jr., and me. "We'd better go inside."

In our makeshift kitchen with its freestanding kerosene stove Guy had us kneel down. "Lord," he prayed, "if this is the end of the world, please take us all to heaven."

We got up and went to the window. There we stood, looking and waiting for whatever was to come. To our great delight, as we watched, the smearing of colors gradually paled and daylight returned. In a matter of minutes, it was all over.

Although newspapers and radios must have forecast the occurrence of the aurora borealis, a rare event in the South, we knew nothing of it.

The hardest thing to get used to at our new home was the noise and activity of the trains. In daytime they rumbled by, trailing smoke and smelling of cinders. The engineer waved down at us from his cab and the flagman bid us goodbye from the caboose. When freight trains stopped to get water, they blocked both roads to our house for long periods of time. Sometimes workmen climbed ladders on the sides of the cars and walked about on the tops. When the train began to move away, the big cars shook, belching steam and lurching forward.

I liked watching passenger trains go by. Strange faces peered out of the windows. Occasionally a hand went up in greeting. Sometimes we saw passengers eating in the dining car. What would it feel like, I wondered, to eat and sleep on a moving train?

Night trains were a different story. The mournful sound of the whistle and the rumble that shook our house jerked me from sleep in terror.

In seventh grade that year, Mrs. Watson nourished my love of books by reading aloud *Swiss Family Robinson*. Her voice painted vivid pictures of the family shipwrecked on an island in the Pacific Ocean.

I was impatient with anyone who did not sit still and listen, for Mrs. Watson always paused when she was interrupted. On one occasion, when a few students grew inattentive, rather than pausing, she brought them to attention another way.

She continued with the story and, maintaining the tone of her reading voice, said, "All who would like a cone of ice cream, please stand by your desk." We had a good laugh when those students did not budge.

Mrs. Watson who always wore a pencil tucked behind one ear, entered me in a reading contest that year. Each student was sent out on the stage of the auditorium, in front of grades five through eleven, to read a passage not seen before. To my delight, I won. I couldn't wait to tell Mamma.

Later, when our principal sent for me to come to the office, I marched down the steps from the second floor with trembling pride. He greeted me, then took a piece of paper from his desk and wrote the word "just." He held it up to me and said, "This is pronounced *just*. You pronounced it *jest*." Disappointed and ashamed, I returned to class.

That year I saw Kleenex for the first time. The box of disposable tissues on the corner of Mrs. Watson's desk seemed a marvelous, if somewhat wasteful, invention.

In winter I suffered my usual bouts of tonsilitis and a cough that hung on, keeping me out of school. During one spell Daddy came home to stay with me while Mamma worked. His cigar, which he rarely lit, was a comforting smell.

At Christmas that year a cousin's grandmother from Columbia came by to see us. She brought me a paper-doll book. Though I sensed she had not realized I'd grown so *big*, I cherished it.

The book's cover was a house. Inside, each page was a room. I pressed out the family of four, their clothes, and their possessions from the back pages. Doors of the closets opened so things could be stored. Drawers of the chests slid from under the heavy pages. Kitchen cabinets had pots I could take out and play with. Everything was so colorful.

I had my make-believe family again like the one Lossie and I created from the Sears, Roebuck catalog. I kept the treasured gift tucked away in my dresser drawer until I was alone. Then I took it out and dreamed of the day I'd have my own family.

# ~55~
# Life Goes On

I was a worrier. I tried to write about my worries in the diary Mamma gave me for Christmas, but the words wouldn't come.

My friendship with Clyde, Jr., meant a great deal to me. Though he could be tough and daring like my other boy cousins, he was kind and sensitive when we were together alone. However, he sometimes had the power to persuade me to act against my better judgment.

One January day we walked home from school to find a

long freight train blocking our way. We waited, hunched over from the biting wind, until our patience grew thin. Finally, Clyde, Jr., said, "Let's climb through."

I thought of the clanging collision of the cars when they started to move.

"You know how long they sit here," he continued, urging me on.

He was right. We wouldn't be able to get home without going all the way back through town, or—

Before I knew it, Clyde, Jr., swung himself up on the couplings. I swallowed to get rid of the dryness in my throat, shifted my books to my left arm, caught hold of the metal handlebar, and pulled up. Suddenly pistons hissed, spraying warm steam onto my bare legs. For a moment I was paralyzed. Quick sounds of movement like muffled rifle shots jarred me, and I jumped free on the other side. I walked the rest of the way on rubbery legs. I would never be so foolish again.

One day just after we arrived home from school we heard a voice over a megaphone. "Go inside," it repeated. "A mad dog is loose. Do not come out until notified." The announcement rippled my arms with goose bumps. I had once seen a mad dog. He foamed at the mouth and ran in circles. Being bitten by one, I knew, meant death.

We waited at our windows. Before long, we heard a gunshot. Once again, the car with the megaphone rolled up and down the streets—this time with an "All's clear."

Another afternoon Clyde, Jr., and I found one of our chickens, freshly killed, on the railroad track. As we'd seen our mothers do, we *dressed* it, cut it up, and fried it. During supper, which our two families often shared, our mothers laughed. The chicken was too tough to eat.

"This was a hen," Mamma explained, "not a fryer. Hens have to be baked in the oven for a long time."

Quilting was one of my interests. On the project I had started, the stitch pattern was "yo-yo." The design was made by hand stitching a thread around the inside circle of a small piece of donut-shaped fabric, then pulling on the thread to draw the material up into a smaller, puffy circle. Afterwards I tacked the yo-yos together end to end to make the complete quilt.

When nobody was around to see him, Clyde, Jr., helped me make yo-yos.

We had not brought our large Atwater Kent radio from the farm but had acquired a small table model shaped like a church. Every afternoon I listened to *Portia Faces Life*. The people on the program became as real to me as those I knew. I could see them in scenes in my mind. If Guy didn't have something better to do, he enjoyed teasing me about the program. He'd unscrew the little receptacle in the light socket where the radio plugged in and put it in his pocket.

"Idella doesn't get to hear what Portia's doing today," he taunted.

He always let me have it just in the nick of time, but I feared he might one day carry out his threat.

As always, I spent much of my time reading. I kept a notebook of things I wanted to remember from my reading. When Jody's father in *The Yearling* told him never to kill an animal unless it was needed for food or it might harm him, I knew I felt that way too.

Even though Uncle Clyde spent much of his time at home with a paperback western curled in his hand, Clyde, Jr., had yet developed the habit of reading for pleasure. He preferred doing physical things. One of his pastimes was throwing a baseball as high as he could and catching it when it plummeted back toward him. Once the ball hit him in the eye. After it healed, that eye had more hazel specks than the other.

I discovered Lloyd Douglas's books that year. *Magnificent Obsession* was my favorite, but I started keeping my diary in the code from *Dr. Hudson's Secret Journal.* I confided to the diary that I did not like my name, Idella. If only I could have been called by my other name, Elizabeth. Clyde, Jr., came nearest to doing that when he started calling me "Aunt Betty." But how I wished he would leave off the "aunt."

Louise was even more of an avid reader than I. Mamma always said, "She keeps her nose in a book." Whenever I tried to talk to her, she looked up from her book reluctantly with an irritated "Huh?" I had to repeat everything I said to her.

The second year we were in Grandma's house, Daddy came home in time for Christmas. On the Saturday before the holiday Mamma drove us to Columbia. We stopped by Grandma's to tell her we were going, and she pressed a dollar bill into each of our hands. I couldn't remember ever owning a whole dollar. We each bought roller skates. On the way home we stopped back by to show them to Grandma. She let us learn to skate in the big hall running the length of her house. She even let us tie pillows to our backsides in case we fell.

Though it was difficult to find a place to skate except on the sidewalks of town, skating became a passion for young people that year. Twine hanging around a person's neck meant a skate key dangled at the end like a charm.

Graduation exercises from elementary school was a big event. With only eleven grades, the eighth was the first year of high school. Our teachers held a party for us in the upstairs of a new peach shed just across the railroad tracks from our school. Mamma made me a pink organdy dress with a sash. She also made me say *yes* to a boy who asked to walk me to the party.

Once there, each girl received a date book. The boys had to go around and ask the girls for "dates." With a little pencil hanging by a string from our book, we signed the boys' names by numbers from one to ten.

"Now remember," our teachers kept repeating, "no boy can have his name in a girl's book more than once."

Books completed, the dating began. A teacher rang a handbell and dates, numbered *one*, got together. We were supposed to talk for ten minutes until the bell jangled again, but I don't remember doing much talking.

My life seemed to be changing fast. The trestle was no longer the frightening place it had been to me as a child. It was now my dreaming place. I sat on the stream bank under the trestle, listening to the water gurgle and thinking about the future and what my life would be like. I still dreamed of becoming a teacher.

I watched Lena, who *took in* wash from the white towns-people at her little house down the way. Unlike Fanny, Lena was tall and reed thin. Her dirt yard lay as clean as a train rail, for sticks and every speck of trash went on the fire beneath her washpot. I liked to see her walk up the narrow road toward town, a basket of freshly ironed laundry balanced on her head.

The sounds and smells of the outdoors took me back to the country. I thought of our home. How sad and lonely it must be. Would this year, I wondered, take us home again?

*Louise, Guy, and Idella, 1941. In background, brown house with vine circling porch swing.*

*Ridge Spring High School basketball team. Betty is holding ball. Louise is on her left.*

*Teachers at Ridge Spring in 1941. Front row: Mrs. Gunter, Mrs. Bonnette. 2nd row: Mrs. Truluck, Mrs. Etta Asbill, Miss Pruit. 3rd row: Miss Bessie, Mrs. Watson, Miss Davis. 4th row: Mr. Murphy, Mr. Marbert, Miss Quatlebaum, Mr. Livingston.*

*Louise, Idella, and Cousin Margie.*

*Guy, 1942.*

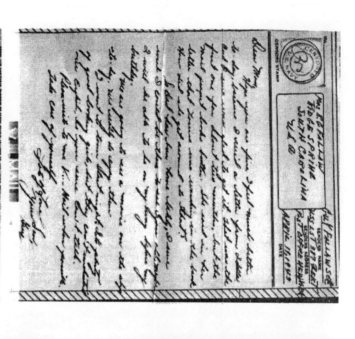

V-mail.

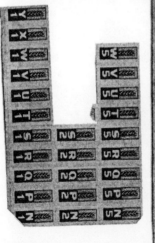

War Ration Stamps.

*Jimmy, 1943, in Army Air Force.*

*Idella, 1943.*

# ~56~
# Home Again

Entering high school made a profound impression on me. I had always loved reading, but my English teacher, Mrs. Bonnette, introduced me to the world of literature. The power of the poetry of Emily Dickinson, Amy Lowell, Edna St. Vincent Millay, Vachel Lindsay, and Robert Frost came alive for me.

When we read *The Rime of the Ancient Mariner*, the parched throat of the man with the albatross around his neck seemed real. His thirst was my thirst.

"Would you please read?" we begged Mrs. Bonnette when struggling readers ruined the rhythm and magic of the piece. Her voice made even *Silas Marner* interesting.

At last I knew what kind of teacher I wanted to be—an English teacher just like Mrs. Bonnette.

With the first nip of fall, Daddy came home again all fired up to move back to the country. He had bought an Ashley Wood Burner, a new kind of wood stove that burned so slowly it kept a fire all night long.

Mamma quit her job, and we returned to the farm. At first everything seemed strange. The fields lay idle. The animals were gone. But before long the rich smells of land and trees, the beloved records of the Edison, and my treasured dolls—though I no longer played with them—became familiar and satisfying. I was home!

On nice days we walked the half mile to Grandma's and

gathered pecans. Inside, she cooked chocolate pudding, and we ate it warm in the kitchen. Afterwards we wandered about in the nearby cemetery. Some of the older tombstones behind the spiked iron fence were blackened with age. In our family plot was the tiny grave of one of Grandma's babies. Grandma had diptheria while she was expecting, and the baby was born dead.

Though Granddaddy and I didn't talk much, we liked sitting in the front yard swing and watching the cars go along the highway. He liked to talk about the boxing matches he'd heard on the radio.

"You mark my word," he said one day as we sat together, "that Joe Louis is gonna hold the world's heavyweight title longer than anybody."

I really didn't like boxing, but I pretended.

"Yep," he'd go on, "that steady two-fisted attack of his gets 'em all sooner or later."

If Daddy's youngest sister, Kathleen, was home, she and I embroidered dresser scarves together. She was pretty, and I wanted to look just like her.

Participating in church activities continued to be important to me. Louise and I were members of the Girls Auxiliary. The GAs, as the group was called, had a leader Mamma didn't care for. Considering herself a good judge of character, Mamma refused to believe that anybody who colored her hair and wore heavy makeup could be a person with morals.

"If you ask me," she said, "anybody that paints her face up like she does has no business teaching a class of girls."

I was trying to understand what she meant when Louise laughed.

"Now you listen to me, young lady," Mamma said with fire in her eyes, as soon as that lesson is over, you and Idella march yourselves right out of there. I'll be waiting out front. I won't have my daughters hanging around the likes of her."

I was already confused about life, but some of Mamma's ideas confused me even more. I couldn't see how makeup could be evil. I looked forward to wearing lipstick.

Our new heater served us well when the winter wind began to howl underneath our house. Before going to bed, we laid our school clothes on a chair near the stove. Mornings, we hurried across cold floors to their comforting warmth.

Often when we left the house, Mamma would say, "We're certainly not leaving things in dying order"— referring to what she considered messy.

I liked to clean. Mamma sometimes called it *plundering*, especially when I got into the trunk. "Mamma," I'd call, "I found a penny."

She'd come back with "Finders keepers. Losers weepers."

Although I was glad for us all to be together on the farm again, things were far from good between Mamma and Daddy. The tension was building. I couldn't bear the arguing. How long would it be, I wondered, before Daddy would leave again. What bothered me most was I knew there was absolutely nothing I could do about it.

## ~57~
## A Special Person

Our soil in the Ridge area was good for growing fruits, especially peaches. I'd studied in geography that in ancient time the ocean washed up as far as the ridge where our town was settled. When the water receded, it left sandy loam on top of the red clay. The soil, along with little chance of late spring frost and continued hot weather during the growing season, made South Carolina a leading peach-growing state.

Once peach blossoms smeared the roadsides with pink, I couldn't wait for the year's crop to come in. At last, this year, I would be old enough to pack peaches.

Louise and I worked at the Steadmans' shed where my seventh grade graduation party took place. The happy voices of workers blended with the noise of flatbed trucks bringing in fruit from orchards. The pungent smell of freshly picked peaches hung in the air.

On an upper level of the shed, *graders* stood ready to snatch the *culls*, peaches not suitable to ship, from a rolling belt. Quick hands tossed them in a center trough. Peaches too soft for shipping went into slatted baskets. Both were sold locally.

Choice peaches followed a path to bins where we girl *ringers* stood ready to pack them into bushel baskets. Our first job was to place a layer of peaches, best side down, in a metal ring on the slanting board before us. Feeling nervous that first day, I leaned into my bin to select the prettiest ones for what would become the top of the basket. Turning the big ring helped to hold the peaches in place. Would I be able to do that and keep the peaches from slipping until I had them all in a tight fit?

With several false starts, I finally got the hang of it. My next step was to place a heavy paper liner in an open-ended, round metal tub. Then I set the tub on top of my ring of peaches. With the ring and the tub below my bin, I pressed a pedal that released peaches to fill the tub. Ever so cautiously I eased the tub up, allowing the paper ring to hold the peaches in place until one of the boy workers came by to slip a bushel shipping basket over it and lift it to the mechanical inverter. With the top of the basket rosy with peaches from the ring, he fastened the top and loaded it into the refrigerated box car waiting along the rails beside the shed.

I was so intent on what I was doing I didn't give a thought to anyone around me. Suddenly I caught a glimpse of a tall, sandy-haired boy I had never seen before. After a while I realized he had been taking my peaches away and supplying me with a ring so I wouldn't lose packing time. Too shy to thank him, I sneaked glances instead. He had the smoothest tanned skin I'd ever seen and dark brown eyes. Once he caught me looking at him and winked at me. I felt my face flush and turned back to my ring of peaches.

The more peaches I packed, the easier the task seemed. I began to look around, taking in the sights and sounds of the shed I had previously blocked out in concentration. Above the hum of the moving belts and voices, the overseer called out orders to the male workers.

Trying not to seem obvious, I looked for the sandy-haired boy. To my surprise, I often found him looking at me. He always winked, and I discovered feelings of pleasure and embarassment flooding through me.

Later in the day we had a break as we waited for more peaches to be brought in from the orchards. I sat by Louise and her friend Betty, whose father owned the shed.

"You see the tall boy loading the peaches in the railroad car?" Betty asked. "That's my cousin, Jimmy Bodie. He's staying with us this summer to work in peaches."

"Where's he from?" Louise asked.

"Batesburg," Betty answered and changed the subject.

The mystery had been solved. I wanted to know more, but I wasn't comfortable asking. I envied Louise her friendship with Betty. They carried on an easy conversation, something I had not yet been able to do. Groups around us made jokes and laughed, calling out to other workers. I sat by, watching, listening, quietly taking it all in.

In an effort to make me talk more, Jimmy began to tease me. One day during a break he handed me a Newgrape soda from the drink machine. "I thought you'd like this," he said. "The bottle's got your shape."

His teasing made me feel more self-conscious and sometimes I pouted. Still, I couldn't hold back my smile when he winked at me across the shed.

Another time as we all sat around waiting for the truck to bring in peaches somebody shouted, "Hey! Let's get in the refrigerated box car and cool off."

Out of sight of the overseer, a crowd of us sneaked into the refreshing coolness. I was standing by Jimmy when a deafening scrape, which ended with a heavy thump, startled me. A prankster had slammed the great sliding door of the railroad car, leaving us in pitch darkness. Jimmy caught my hand.

Whether the screams sounded an alarm or the overseer missed us, I don't know; but the door opened, bringing us face to face with an angry supervisor.

"I don't have time to get to the bottom of this," he barked. "It just better not happen again." With a fling of his arm toward the bins, he added, "Peaches are waiting."

Each ringer had a small white card with her assigned number on it. Before we placed the peaches, we laid a card in the ring so the bookkeeper could keep an account of how many we packed. One week I made eight dollars. It seemed like a fortune.

I hated for peach season to end. Even though Batesburg was only nine miles away, I knew I probably would not get to see Jimmy until the next summer. I wanted to write to him, but I dared not. Girls never contacted boys. All I could do was add Jimmy to my world of dreams.

# ~58~
# The Green House

"Mamma," I pleaded, "do we have to move here?" We stood before a rental house in Ridge Spring. "It's the ugliest house I've ever seen."

Mamma acted as if she hadn't heard my question. "Did you see the blackberry bushes out back?" she asked.

The sickly green house sat up on high pillars. I could see all the way underneath it to the backyard.

Louise burst through the front door. "Boy, there'll be some draft in this big hall when the weather gets cold."

I had the feeling Mamma didn't like the house either, but we had to live in town. Daddy needed the car to look for work, and we wouldn't be able to get back and forth from the country.

Now that Guy had graduated from high school, he lived in Columbia and worked in an uncle's store. I missed him.

In this move we left only a few of our possessions behind at the farm. Mamma stored them in mine and Louise's bedroom in case she decided to rent the house. I couldn't bear to think of another family living there.

Did Louise mind moving, I wondered. She and I never discussed our feelings with one another. At least the move would bring her close to her friend Betty. They could visit after school.

After we got settled into the green house, Mamma went back to work. Louise and I were put in charge of the house. One did the grocery shopping, cooked supper, and cleaned the kitchen. The other kept the rest of the house. Each week we swapped chores. For doing a good job Mamma gave us each fifty cents a week.

I'd always loved to sew. That year I began to make my own clothes. I made a peasant blouse with lace around the neck, a gathered skirt, and a brown and white striped seersucker dress.

Since I enjoyed singing, I became a member of chorus at school. The phrase "amber waves of grain" in the song "America the Beautiful" always brought to mind the days on our farm when rippling fields of grain stretched across the land like a golden ocean. In the breeze the movement of the grain resembled waves. I thought of the sights and sounds of harvest when giant machines knifed through the fields, cutting and threshing the wheat.

Mrs. Truluck, our chorus director, worked hard with us, teaching songs like "To the King and Beautiful Dreamer." She would stand by the piano, one hand on a key to give us the pitch, the other poised to bring down for a synchronizing start. In the spring our chorus went to Columbia to perform for the State Teachers' Convention.

I also became a member of the basketball team although I was far too self-conscious to be a good player. Louise was a team star. We practiced and played our games on outdoor courts.

Autograph books became the rage at school. Mine was red with AUTOGRAPHS stamped in gold across the cover. It held swinging little verses like

> *If I was a postcard,*
> *I'll tell you what I'd do.*
> *I'd buy myself a one cent stamp*
> *And mail myself to you.*

> *If you see a mule tied to a tree,*
> *Pull his tail and think of me.*

> *When I die, don't bury me at all.*
> *Just pickle my bones in Ridge Spring High School hall.*
> *Lay an arithmetic book under my chin*
> *And tell Mr. Marbert I'm still staying in.*

In her fun-loving way, Louise wrote

> *Cream in the pitcher;*
> *Milk in the bowl.*
> *I can't catch a fellow*
> *To save my soul.*

But she did have fellows. Boys liked talking with Louise. When they tried talking to me, I never could think of anything to say.

Mamma was right about the blackberry vine. It was a bright spot at the ugly green house. At my turn to cook, I braved the stickers and picked enough for a pie. We missed the topping of Bittersweet's rich cream.

During the time we lived in town, Louise and I hurried through our lessons and chores so we could read. That summer our town opened its first library in a room over the bank.

"I'm going to read every book in the library," Louise announced. I joined her. With doors and windows flung open to catch breezes, we nestled down in our big overstuffed chairs. I read Jack London's *Call of the Wild* and felt the chill of the Yukon. I explored the Wild West with Zane Grey in *Riders of the Purple Sage*. I went through Bess Streeter Aldrich's books and vowed if I ever had a little girl, I would name her Susanne like the girl in *Song of Years*. In evenings Mamma read too. She liked Grace Livingston Hill's books.

Looking back at our time in the green house, I don't think of its ugliness. Instead, I remember my reading chair and the journeys I took through wonderful books.

# ~59~
# The Brown House

"Oh, no! Not again." This time it was Louise who protested. Mamma was moving us, but not back to the farm.

By now Grandma and Granddaddy were back in their home in town. A small brown house next door to them had become vacant. We would rent that, Mamma told us.

We moved in early summer. A morning glory vine trailing up taut strings between the porch pillars comforted me. It wrapped around the swing side of the porch like a cocoon. The swing became my reading place.

For the first time Guy would not be heading off to school

with Louise and me.

On one of his quick trips by the house, Daddy brought a typewriter. For Louise and me it was a dream come true. In spite of sticking keys, we pecked away strugglng to write poetry like Emily Dickinson and Elizabeth Barrett Browning. Thinking of Jimmy, I memorized the sonnet "How Do I Love Thee."

Mrs. Bonnette sent one of Louise's poems to be considered for a state anthology. It was published. Louise collected her poems in a notebook. "Okay," she'd say when Eleanor, a friend who lived up the street, came over, "if you want to hear poetry, gather 'round."

We'd sit on the floor in the living room while she read her poems on death and lost love in her saddest voice. When she finally made us cry, she shut her notebook and hopped up. "That's it," she said and marched off to something else.

Mrs. Bonnette continued to be my English teacher throughout high school. Among the Classics, I found Willa Cather. In her youth she moved from Virginia to Nebraska. In writing about her own feeling of loss in leaving her home, she authored *My Antonia*. Antonia's family left Bohemia to come to America's Midwest. I found a kindred spirit in the book's heroine.

I loved the memory work in English class, especially Shakespeare's *Romeo and Juliet*. I liked the romantic books like Emily Bronte's *Wuthering Heights*. I avidly read *Gone with the Wind* and couldn't wait to see the movie. Shirley Temple had long ago been replaced as my idol by Ginger Rogers and Fred Astaire. I was enraptured by their romantic dance movies.

Even though I didn't wear makeup in public, I liked to experiment with it at home. I burned matches and made mascara to make my lashes look longer. I polished my nails and fussed over my hair. I became distressed when my hair wouldn't do right. The cowlick at my forehead was especially hard to control.

Catchy little lyrics like those in "Chattanooga Choo Choo," "Elmer's Tune," "Three Little Fishes," and "Flat Foot Floogie" stuck in my mind. But I preferred slow songs like "Blueberry Hill" and "Sentimental Journal."

Trains that had been grumbling monsters, reeking with the smell of coal and darkening the air with soot, now stirred new feelings in me. The lonesome call of the whistle beckoned me to faraway places.

Because I was eager to learn all I could about boy/girl relationships, I was excited to hear that our young minister's wife would speak to our youth group on "The Problems of Growing Up." The program was to include "petting," the current expression for hugging and kissing.

Eager listeners filled the chairs that Sunday evening. When Mrs. Owens finally got to the part we waited for, she paused, looking deep in thought. Then she said, "Petting." The silence grew. She gave a deep sigh before concluding, "Young people, just let me say that petting jeopardizes your future." Then she moved on to the next topic. I am sure others felt as letdown as I did, but no one said a word.

I remember hurrying home that night to look up *jeopardize* in our dictionary. All these years later I realize Mrs. Owens gave us some good advice. But I wish she had been more open with us. I'm sure there were others in the group, like me, who wanted to hear about "life" from someone we respected.

In spite of having to plow my way through higher mathematics, school continued to be the center of my life. As juniors, we were already being allowed special privileges. During lunch we went on the stage in the auditorium and danced the Big Apple. Laura, a senior, brought her record player. She called out the dance moves as we trucked to the center of the circle and back again to the tune of "Roll Out the Barrel."

In the spring of that year Mrs. Bonnette sponsored a trip to Washington, D. C., for juniors and seniors. Most of the students had never been out of South Carolina. A few of us had seen the mountains of North Carolina and traveled to Augusta, Georgia. The sights and sounds of big cities amazed and thrilled us all.

I couldn't sleep the first night in Richmond, Virginia. The activity outside our hotel window was unlike any I had ever heard. Car motors raced and horns honked. It was much more disturbing than the night train thundering through our little town.

In addition to all the historical sights in Washington, we joined other visitors in a moonlight cruise on the Potomac River.

"Go up on third deck," classmates whispered in passing.

There to my surprise people were petting up a storm. "We need to get Mrs. Owens up here to tell them the *jeopardy* they're in," I heard Louise say.

Just before school was out that year, the seniors initiated juniors into the Beta Club, then called the National Honor Society.

"All right," the president said, "you heard the rules and regulations. Now all you have to do to be a member is be initiated. You must swallow a raw oyster and drink a glass of buttermilk. Follow me."

With a sinking feeling, I moved with the others to the kitchen of the home where the meeting was being held. The buttermilk was fine. I was a farm girl. But the raw oyster! I couldn't do it. All the others had followed orders. I just stood there feeling as if I was about to be hanged.

Finally, Mrs. Bonnette said, "Just drop the oyster in your buttermilk, Idella, and drink it down." I did.

That evening I did not watch fireflies from the porch or enjoy the night air. I lay on my bed sick to my stomach, all the while vowing, "I'll never eat another oyster as long as I live."

# ~60~
# A Year to Remember

I had seen Jimmy only once since the previous summer. That was in a Batesburg store where he worked on Saturdays and after school. Then shyness seemed to be contagious as we tried to talk to each other in front of Mamma, Louise, and the adult workers. I wanted peach season to hurry and begin so we would be working in the shed together. When it finally did, it was more than I dreamed for.

"How about riding to Columbia with me tonight?" Jimmy asked above the chatter and clacking of machinery. "I'm going to drive a truckload of peaches to the Farmers' Market for Mr. Boatwright."

"I'll ask Mamma," I told him.

In all the time Jimmy and I had known each other, we had never been alone together. I was fifteen, and if this was a date, it was my first. It didn't seem to matter to Jimmy that I didn't talk much. We just bumped along in the truck enjoying each other's company.

We arrived at the big outdoor market at dusk. At first the place appeared deserted. Then we spotted a man sitting on a table under the covered area. He pulled himself up, took a drag on his cigarette and tossed it on the ground. "Been wondering when I was gonna git them peaches for in the morning," he barked and followed that with a curse word.

Jimmy had one leg out of the truck when I heard him say, "Watch how you talk. I got my girlfriend with me."

His words rippled over me like a sweet song.

When peach season was over, Jimmy left for Maryland to pick tomatoes. He wrote to me and signed his letter "I love you."

That summer, for the first time, Louise and I went alone to Gaston. Our visits had been gradually changing. The younger boys were growing out of their peskiness and life with them was calmer. We still loved swimming. Each afternoon we wriggled into our wool bathing suits that had not dried from the previous day and headed for the mill pond. Louise swam with the boys beneath the cascading tumble of the spillway, but Margie and I were more cautious.

We did, though, on a different occasion, join Louise behind the Macks' bathhouse for the daring experience of smoking rabbit tobacco.

Another day the three of us locked ourselves in their new bathroom and took down Aunt Frances's nursing book from the shelf. We had been hovering over it trying to learn "the facts of life," when Louise said, "Shoot fire! I can't even tell what they're talking about. The drawings don't even make sense."

I thought about my friend Ethelyn's attempts to educate me, and my stomach stirred in a strange uneasiness. Why was it so hard for young people to find out what adults knew?

Then Margie had an idea. "Let's go upstairs and read the

letters Mamma got from Aunt Grace when she was teaching on the coast."

I followed along, not at all sure what we would learn about life from letters Mamma wrote before she was married. I had seen them in the bottom dresser drawer in Margie's room and once mentioned them to Mamma.

Mamma had laughed and turned to Aunt Frances. "Frank, why don't you burn those things up?" Then she said solemnly, "Wish I'd known then what I know now."

"Don't say that, Grace." As always, Aunt Frances's voice was soft. "You wouldn't have your children."

Mamma jerked her head toward me as if she'd forgotten I was there. "Go on, Dell," she said, "and play."

I felt funny reading Mamma's letters. In a way it was like trespassing. "Grady's coming down in his new car this weekend," she'd written in her looped letters. "Maybe we'll come up to the homeplace to see you."

"Hey," Louise said, "you know that metal shoe buttoner at home? Listen to this."

"You've just got to see my new shoes," she read aloud. "It takes me forever to get them buttoned up in the mornings. I couldn't do it at all without my button hook. They do pinch the sides of my big toes when I've taught in them all day, but I wear them anyway."

The one I was holding read, "Grady says I talk too much. Ha! He must like me anyway. He keeps coming back."

It was Mamma's voice all right. Even if she hadn't signed it, I'd know who wrote it. But it made me sad. If only they still loved each other like that. I folded my letter and replaced it in the envelope. "I'm going to pick scuppernongs," I said.

The yellow light of evening fell over the arbor and

blended with the smell of ripening fruit. Suddenly I was transported back to the days when we were little children and dashed about the yard giggling. Was this how getting older felt?

In late July a terrible epidemic occurred: polio. People were stricken with a stiffness in the neck and back and had difficulty moving. Some became permanently paralyzed. A teenager from Batesburg was among the victims. I could hear panic in adult voices as they spoke of it. Lakes closed to swimmers. Movie theaters shut their doors. Fear that the disease would spread mirrored in faces.

Our church took up money for an iron lung victim. I went with others from our church to Columbia to visit the patient. For many days, especially at night, what I had seen and heard haunted me. Only the young woman's head was visible outside the great iron chamber encasing her body. She could not turn her head but looked at us through a mirror hanging above her face. A monstrous hissing, like the breath of a giant, pushed and pulled air in and out of the machine as it breathed for her.

From the front bedroom of the little brown house, my nightly prayers were more earnest than ever. What if someone in my family contracted polio? What if Jimmy did?

# ~61~
# Shocking News

Thankfully, the polio epidemic had subsided by the time school opened for my senior year. Though Louise had talked of being a doctor, she postponed college and took a job in our bank.

Throughout high school Louise had bitten her nails. Now she determined to break the habit. I offered her fingernail polish, but she would have none of it, except to stop a run in her stockings. She chose "the white-glove cure." She wore the gloves when she read or went to the movies. At night she slept in them.

I envied Louise the natural curl in her auburn hair. We both wore our hair shoulder length, but I had to roll mine and pin it with bobby pins each night to make it have curl, which was the style of the time.

Mrs. Bonnette continued to spur my desire to be an English teacher through our study of works like Walter Scott's "Lady of the Lake" and George Eliot's *Adam Bede* and *Mill on the Floss*. I found it hard to believe it was considered improper for women to write for the public in the 1800s. Because this was true, Mary Ann Evans used a man's name—George Eliot—on her books.

I had created the perfect college in my imagination. Judging from the catalog in our school library, Mars Hill Junior College near Asheville, North Carolina, came nearest to what I had imagined. I liked the pictures of buildings nestled in mountains and the ivy-covered stone library.

In afternoons when I wasn't studying or sitting at the trestle watching clouds drift like white scarfs across the sky, I took walks with my friend Eleanor. Usually we went through town where we bought a Snickers bar for five cents. We had a great time together, laughing, often making our own kind of southern talk.

"Did you see that whatcha-ma-call-it?" she'd ask.

I'd come back with "You mean the thing-a-ma-jig?"

Sometimes Eleanor's brother, Emory, and Clyde, Jr., joined us. Though Jimmy was always in my thoughts, I seldom saw him because he lived nine miles away and his family did not have a car. Occasionally we double dated for a movie.

On Sunday evening, December 7, 1941, I entered our church's youth group meeting to hear the most shocking news of my life: the Japanese had bombed Pearl Harbor! The surprise attack drew America into World War II. President Franklin Delano Roosevelt made the declaration of war.

In a matter of days a wave of patriotism spread over our country. Young men enlisted in various branches of the service. Guy joined the Navy.

Although hard times had taught thriftiness, people began to scrimp and save with new vigor. No sacrifice was too great for our men in uniform who risked their lives for their country. Everything went toward the war effort. We wrapped bits of string and aluminum foil—even the thin foil under wrapping from chewing gum—into balls. Scrap drives brought in metal to be melted down for weapons. Those who could afford to do so bought war bonds.

The government set up a system of rationing. At the top of the list was gasoline, which sold for eighteen cents a gallon. Tires were no longer available except in the cases of proven need. Many cars were put up on blocks. "Is this trip necessary?" was posted in public places.

As did every other family, we received a book of ration stamps. With the purchase of meat, sugar, coffee, and other staples, the merchant removed the appropriate stamp. He was then required to keep an accurate account for the government.

Even shoes were rationed. Although they sold for only $1.50 to $2.00, they were hard to find.

With so many men away from home, factories needed workers. For the first time women wore long pants in public as they took over jobs formerly held by men.

Nurses were needed to care for the wounded. Women joined the WACS (Women's Auxiliary Army Corps) and WAVES (Women's Appointed Volunteer Emergency Service), branches of the armed services set up for them.

With six weeks of basic training, our young men were sent to battlefields. Guy's ship sailed from Norfolk, Virginia.

Each evening we gathered around the radio for news about the war. Walter Winchell opened his broadcast with a clicking that sounded like Morse code. Then came "Good evening, Mr. and Mrs. North America, and all the ships at sea. Let's go to press."

We held our breaths for Edward R. Murrow's report from London, where many of our soldiers were stationed. England was being attacked by Germany. From New York, a voice said "Calling Edward R. Murrow. Come in, Mr. Murrow." We breathed a sigh of relief when we heard him drag out "This . . . is London." We knew then that, at least for one more day, England was still in the fight.

Newsreels at the movies brought scenes of the war. German soldiers raised their arms in the Nazi pledge of "Heil Hitler!" to their mustached dictator. President Roosevelt, his familiar long cigarette holder in hand, sat beside Winston Churchill smoking his cigar. On the battlefield, Ernie Pyle and other journalists crawled in foxholes to interview fighting men so they could accurately describe the war for newspaper readers back home.

At home we kept blackout material handy to hang over windows when notified. Our town had "lights out" practices, when everything lay in complete darkness. Fearing the war might come to America, night sounds of planes caused us to douse lights or cover windows.

Convoys of trucks and jeeps with servicemen filled the highways. Cars stopped as they would for a funeral possession to let them pass. Passenger trains now transported troops rather than pleasure seekers. Day after day trains passed our house loaded with uniformed men. We waved to them from our yard.

At night the rocking of troop-filled trains pulled me from sleep. I raised up to see moonlight reflecting off railway cars wending their way into the darkness. The click-clack of steel hitting steel kept rhythm with the beat of my heart. Finally, the last car flung faint sparks that flew away into the night. Always I said a prayer for Guy and our boys in combat.

# ~62~
# Home Fires

Soon, most men in our town had gone to war. Except for older males, those in bad health, and a few hardship cases— situations where their families or farms needed them—every man had either volunteered or been drafted.

Daddy, as many men of his age group, had gone to work at the shipyard in Charleston. All worked long hours for the war effort. He rarely got home.

Although the location of soldiers and sailors overseas was top secret, we wrote to our boys. With special stationery, called V-mail, we sent letters for overseas to an army post office in the United States. Before they were forwarded, the letters were photocopied, reducing them in size for shipment because of the large volume of mail.

All letters were censored. Sometimes words, lines, or even whole paragraphs of those coming to us from the soldiers were blacked out. No locations or military information could be disclosed.

Our letters seemed to keep up the soldiers' morale. Servicemen gave their buddies addresses of friends and relatives back home so they would receive more letters. Write we did—for writing was a show of patriotism.

By spring Guy was on a ship in the Mediterranean Sea. We learned this from a letter that said, "Today we played baseball in Algiers." The censor let that one slip.

Sacrificing personal needs and taking the time to write letters was looked upon as keeping the home fires burning. We were proud of our men. Anybody who acted in the least unpatriotic—like using gasoline to ride around for pleasure or trying to get extra ration stamps—was asked "Don't you know there's a war going on?"

In spite of our worries, we had to carry on with usual activities at school and church. At school the pledge of allegiance to the flag became a solemn occasion. Many of the students' fathers and brothers were away in service.

I was pleased to get the part of the lady of the house in our senior play, "The Meddlesome Maid." My long-time friend from first grade, Margaret Ellen, was my maid. The long practice sessions and fellowship helped take my mind off the war. I liked being on stage. I put myself in the skin of the person I played. I had no need to be shy. I was not myself.

The church kept our faith strong. The world situation brought about an early maturity in young people. I could feel it in myself and my friends. I began to look at others in a different light.

After the senior play, Miss Bessie, my stern second-grade teacher put her arm around my shoulder and said, "I'm hearing good things about you, Idella." How differently I had seen her when I was young. I couldn't help believing I was the one who had changed.

Another incident with a teacher gave me insight into human nature. Our annual mother–daughter banquet was held in the school's large home economics room. Mamma was asked to speak on "What My Daughters Mean to Me." I was proud of her.

Afterwards, my friend Rachel and I looked for our teacher, Miss Hendrix, to help her with the cleanup. We found her outside the door on the kitchen steps, crying. Rachel dropped down beside her and asked, "What's wrong?"

"I—I forgot to put the pickles on the plates," she sobbed.

It was the first time I had ever seen a teacher cry. From then on I realized that everyone has a sensitive side though they may not show it. I saw too what pressure our teacher had been under with the responsibility of the banquet. Above all, I learned that things are not always as they appear to be to *me* at the moment.

The home economics room was also the site of our junior–senior banquet. This time the large space was transformed into a southern garden in late evening. Pink roses climbed trellises. Blue crepe paper dotted with stars became the sky. That garden was an enchanting place. Only students from our school could attend so my friend Emory was my escort.

Graduation was formal, as always. I sat on the stage, waiting to give the salutatory address. My chief memory of the entire event is one of physical misery. A bobby pin holding my cap in place gouged my head. I dared not touch it for fear I would loosen the mortar board and it would fall onto the stage.

Summer was upon us once more and, with school over, the war again monopolized our thoughts. I signed up to work in the Peach Association's shipping office. I missed being at the peach shed with Jimmy, but the office job paid more and I needed the extra money for college. With my salary and the $100 loan from my school, I could pay the tuition and board of $250 for my first year at Mars Hill.

Jimmy and I did get to be together more often in evenings. He had his mind made up about two things: he was going to join the Air Force as soon as he became eighteen, and he wanted me to wait for him to come home. I promised him I would wait.

Because of the war, we were all learning about other cultures. A friend of Louise's sent her a grass skirt from Hawaii. We listened to "Blue Hawaii" on the radio and danced the hula. Robert Mack, the cousin from Gaston who was such a tease as a boy, mailed Louise and me silk stockings from Japan. Although they were a red raw silk, we prized them. Stockings had become hard to get, as nylon was needed for the war effort. Since all stockings at that time had seams up the back, some girls drew lines on their legs with an eyebrow pencil to make it appear they had on hose. Going barelegged, especially when dressing up, was not considered good taste.

Lists of deaths of servicemen in the newspaper grew longer with each passing week. We all feared for our boys. If a mother lost a son, she was considered a gold-star mother for having made the ultimate sacrifice for her country. We heard of a mother in the upstate who lost both her sons.

The government notified families of those killed in action by telegram. In June when a telegram came to our house, we knew the news was bad. It read, "The Secretary of War expresses deep regret that your son, Guy Denham Fallaw, is missing in action."

My heart fluttered wildly in my chest like a captured bird beating its wings against its cage. *My brother was missing.*

# ~63~
# A New Beginning

Long, troop-filled trains continued to grind their way cross-country. Other things were changing—some of them not for the best. Our little town was no longer friendly to those who were not native to the area. In wartime *certain people* could be spies. A German merchant who had owned a store in Ridge Spring for many years was suddenly shunned by townspeople as a matter of loyalty to the United States, since our country was at war with Germany.

Prison camps popped up near Ridge Spring and other neighboring small towns. German prisoners worked on farms and in peach orchards. Their labor replaced that previously provided by our men who were away fighting. In passing, I caught glimpses of the prisoners— young, tall, blonde, blue-eyed. How did it feel, I wondered, to be in a foreign country where no one spoke your language? Could Guy be a prisoner of war in another land? I could not hate these men.

With our country at war, Guy missing in action, and my plans set to leave home for the first time, I became increasingly anxious. Had I made a mistake in choosing a college so far away? I would not be able to return home until Christmas holidays.

I took long walks down the railroad to sit at the trestle and think. How life had changed since we looked for signs of gnomes along those same tracks!

One day Louise received a letter from a sailor on Guy's ship. "I am sorry to tell you," he wrote, "but Guy was killed when our ship was torpedoed."

Our hope was shattered!

Another letter came—from Charleston. It was from Daddy. He had learned about Guy. "Grace," it read, "I want you to know that I have always loved you and the kids."

My trunk was packed. Skirts and blouses for classes. For Sundays, a blue velvet dress and my shell pin to wear at the neck. A white wool hat Mamma crocheted. A brown tweed suit and a heavy coat for the mountain winter. Three pairs of shoes—brown leather pumps for dress, saddle oxfords for school, and knee-high boots for deep snows. And, a blue "fascinator," the rage of the times. This lightweight, loosely woven scarf was long enough to go over my head and cross at the neck. One end fell softly in front; the other lay over my shoulder. The cozy warmth would protect against the biting mountain air.

Our country had been at war nine months when I left for Mars Hill Junior College. I boarded an early-morning Greyhound bus at the filling station in town. With the coach motor still running, the driver slid my trunk into the luggage compartment. I stood engulfed in the smell of gas fumes and said goodbye to Mamma and Louise.

·My insides flip-flopped as I found a vacant seat. The

motor revved and sped away. I did not need to look back to know that my hometown and everything I was familiar with was growing farther and farther away from me.

For months afterwards my stomach churned with homesickness. As always, I turned to books. I spent hours in the ivy-covered library, often browsing in the upstairs stacks. There I saw my old friends—Jane Eyre, Heathcliff, Antonia, and others whose plights had been heartrending. Crying for their sorrows gave me an opportunity to weep for myself.

It was also there I discovered Thomas Wolfe and his *Look Homeward, Angel* in which he shared his agony of leaving his Asheville home to go to college.

Mamma wrote that the War Department had confirmed what we already knew about Guy and sent his Purple Heart. He had been killed in the invasion of Sicily.

Reading, the kindness of my teachers, friendships, and letters from home sustained me until Christmas and carried me closer to my goal of becoming an English teacher.

By spring of my freshman year almost all of the male students had "joined up." Jimmy did too and was sent to the China–Burma–India theater with the Flying Tigers of the Fourteenth Air Force. Our letters flew back and forth across the miles. I wore his wings and took comfort in our songs, "You'll Never Know" and "I'll Walk Alone."

By the time I graduated from junior college and enrolled in the all-girls Columbia College in Columbia, South Carolina, Mamma and Louise had returned to the farm, the place I always thought of as home.

One day in 1945 I was in the chemistry lab on the third floor of the college where I struggled to determine what elements and compounds a sample contained. Suddenly shouts from below grabbed my attention. Girls were screaming, "The war is over! The war is over!"

The boys who had not given their lives would be coming home. I was thankful Jimmy was one of them. Now, he and I would fulfill our promise to spend our future together.

# Epilogue

I fulfilled my dream of marrying Jimmy and becoming an English teacher. During the years I was teaching and caring for our children, I continued to nourish my love of words by reading and keeping notebooks and journals. Now as a writer I draw on many of those captured experiences that might otherwise have been forgotten.

Although I did not realize it when I was growing up, watching and listening to life about me gave me insight into the way people feel and act. It also sharpened my skill of keen observation, which is absolutely necessary to a writer.

Many of my personal experiences, embellished or altered with imagination, appear in my fiction and nonfiction. After reading *Carolina Girl*, perhaps you can see glimpses of my life that have become parts of my books.

# Glossary

**bloomers**
loose trousers gathered at the ankles; worn in late 1800s by girls for athletics

**blued**
process of whitening clothes with a chemical substance

**brooder house**
heated shelter for raising young chicks

**buncher**
a measured container for holding cut asparagus to be tied into bundles for sale

**butchering**
slaughtering animals for meat

**B.V.D.**
a trademark of underwear

**"chitlins"**
chitterlings; the small intestines of hogs fried to a crisp

**corncrib**
section of barn for storing ears of corn

**corset**
lady's girdle stiffened with pieces of bone

**crackling cornbread**
bread made of meal with crisply fried bits of skin added

**croker bag**
a bag made of coarse material like burlap

**cured**
manner of preserving meat by salting and smoking

**depression**
a period of history marked by widespread unemployment; America's "Great Depression" began with the stock market crash in October 1929 and continued through 1930s.

**dinner**
term used for main midday meal

**dogwood broom**
yard broom made by fastening small branches of a dogwood tree together with twine or wire

**dressed**
process of preparing an animal for cooking by removing all parts that are not edible

**dry goods store**
an old-time store selling cloth, clothes, and sewing notions

**filling station**
gas station providing full service

**fodder shock**
cornstalks stacked on end to cure and dry for animals' food

**freak**
a person or animal who is different, physically or mentally, from what is considered normal

**graders**
workers in a peach packing shed who determined whether peacheswere suitable for shipping

# Glossary

**grip**
old-time word for suitcase

**gypsy**
persons who move about from place to place in nomad style

**ice box**
old-time refrigerator; an insulated cabinet used for cooling food with a partition for ice in the upper section

**ice house**
place where ice was made and sold in huge blocks

**jawbreaker**
a large ball of hard candy

**Model A**
Ford car popular in early 1930s; Ford's third car

**nail keg**
wooden barrel nails were shipped and stored in

**parlor**
old-time word for living room

**picture show**
old-time word for movie

**pie safe**
a wooden kitchen cabinet for storing food, especially pies and bread

**rock salt**
coarse salt that aids quicker freezing

**September gale**
a cool wind in late summer

**singletree**
a wooden bar swinging freely at the front of a wagon or plow to which a horse's traces were attached

**slips**
in this case, plant cuttings

**slop**
kitchen waste used for feeding pigs

**smokehouse**
a building where meats are smoked in order to preserve and flavor

**souse**
a pickled food made from the feet, ears, and head of a hog

**still**
crude homemade apparatus for making illegal liquor

**sugar tit**
homemade baby's pacifier

**switch**
a thin twig used in punishing children

**twenties bob**
a short haircut popular for women in the 1920s

**traces**
chains or straps connecting an animal's harness to the plow or wagon it is pulling

## ABOUT THE AUTHOR:

Idella Fallaw Bodie taught English for more than thirty years. She retired from South Aiken High School, where she served for many years as chairperson of the English Department. There, she also taught creative writing and sponsored the school's literary magazine, Calliope.

Mrs. Bodie's first book was published in 1971. *Carolina Girl* is her twelfth. She is currently busy on a series of biographies of heroes and heroines of the American Revolution. Although most of her books are works of fiction, so much history is included that South Carolina teachers are able to incorporate these, as well as her nonfiction, into their curriculums.

With her husband Jim, Idella Bodie lives in Aiken, South Carolina, about forty minutes from the farm on which she grew up. She spends as much time as possible writing and researching upcoming projects. But her schedule continues to stay filled with speaking engagements and writing workshops.

- Additional information can be obtained from reference books, including *Something About the Author*.

- Idella Bodie's books are available through local libraries and bookstores.

## BOOKS BY IDELLA BODIE:

<u>*NOVELS:*</u>

GHOST IN THE CAPITOL
"... a frightening, fun-filled adventure."—*Evening Post* (Charleston, SC)

THE MYSTERY OF EDISTO ISLAND
"Bodie handles suspense especially well, and readers over the age of 9 will be turning pages frantically to find out what happens in the next chapter."  —*Georgia Guardian* (Savannah, GA)

THE MYSTERY OF THE PIRATE'S TREASURE
"... a most interesting mystery story for the 10 to 14 set."
—*Aiken Standard* (Aiken, SC)

THE SECRET OF TELFAIR INN
"... the mystery is intriquing, parts are shivery and the end is satisfying with all loose ends tied neatly."
—*Herald-Journal* (Spartanburg, SC)

STRANDED!
"[Bodie] manages to create a story full of stirring action, and, at the same time, deals sensitively with the practical and moral aspects of capital punishment and loyalty to friends and parents."
—*Citizen-News* (Asheville, NC)

TROUBLE AT STAR FORT
"Fun and educational for preteens."  —*Sandlapper* Magazine

WHOPPER
"... honest and engaging, but with no comments or episodes that would rob a child of his childhood."  —*Guideposts*

<u>*BIOGRAPHIES:*</u>

A HUNT FOR LIFE'S EXTRAS:
*The Story of Archibald Rutledge*
"Rutledge was a unique South Carolinian—a combination outdoorsman, conservationist and man of letters. Bodie has captured his essence in a study which makes the reader wish for more."
—*Sun News* (Myrtle Beach, SC)

## THE MAN WHO LOVED THE FLAG
". . . a concise biography for elementary-school students of Sgt. William Jasper, one of South Carolina's Revolutionary War heroes. . . . Bodie writes a descriptive account about Jasper's life, highlighting his dedication to freedom and his country's flag." —*Carologue* (S. C. Historical Society)

## SOUTH CAROLINA WOMEN
". . . an excellent addition to a home or school library."
—*Sun News* (Myrtle Beach, SC)

## *GHOST STORIES:*

## GHOST TALES FOR RETELLING
"Kids and parents alike will enjoy reading or hearing the scary yarns Bodie related so well." —*The Pilot* (Southern Pines, NC)

## *ACTIVITIES GUIDES:*

An activities guide to *Trouble at Star Fort* and a creative writing guide to *Whopper* are available to teachers using these books in their classrooms.

## *UPCOMING:*

THE SECRET MESSAGE, the story of teenaged Revolutionary War heroine Emily Geiger, is scheduled for release September 1, 1998.

---

For information on individual Idella Bodie books or accompanying guides, call Sandlapper Publishing Co., Inc., 1-800-849-7263.